Accuracy

*A Guide to Living Skillfully
and Successfully in
Today's Crazy Times*

PHILIP "SHARP SKILLS" JACOBS

A REBEL Firm Book
A Division of REBEL Firm

Order this book online at www.trafford.com
or email orders@trafford.com

Most Trafford titles are also available at major online book retailers.

Cover design by Cory Wright of DPI Worx
Edited by Ashley Ratcliff
Photography by Char Beck of Char Beck Photography

Printed in the United States of America.

ISBN: 978-1-4907-4646-3 (sc)
ISBN: 978-1-4907-4645-6 (e)

Trafford rev. 09/18/2014

 www.trafford.com

North America & international
toll-free: 1 888 232 4444 (USA & Canada)
fax: 812 355 4082

To my wife, Menzelle, and my son, Philip Jr., you are my motivation to become more accurate each day.

TABLE OF CONTENTS

Section II
Relationships

Section III
Finances, Occupation, Business and Entrepreneurship

Section IV
Health and Goals

ACKNOWLEDGEMENTS

This book would not have been possible without the small army of people who gathered around me to produce it. I would like to thank the following individuals who invested their resources into my vision to make it a reality:

Char Beck, Charlett Shoecraft, Christina Kemp, Erin Croteau, Danny Morledge, Elliot Fauske, Dr. Gloria Morrow, Gwendolyn Phillips Coates, Heidi Whittenberg, Karen Altus, LaNicia Williams, Menzelle Jacobs, Randy Thomas, Severina Britto, Shirley Noble, Stephanie Williams, Steven Wayne and Tyler Gorsiline — it would require another book for me to express my gratitude to each of you.

I would like to thank Ashley Ratcliff for her superb editing skills on this project, Cory Wright for his excellent graphics design work and Char Beck for the top-notch photography. You all are worth double your weight in gold.

Lastly, I would like to thank Trafford Publishing for guiding me throughout this journey, helping me stay on track, and the relentless follow-up.

Foreword

P hilip "Sharp Skills" Jacobs in *Accuracy* helps us see that the best way to make our dreams come true is to wake up. To grow up. The essential key is to look up. We understand that 96 percent of Americans believe in God, yet 50 percent will say, "I'm spiritual, but I'm not religious." Thus, too many lives are inaccurate, lacking a proper orientation toward God to empower them to become *accurate*.

Jacobs spells out in itemized detail how areas such as health, vision, self-imaging, relationships, occupation and goal setting are the divine recipe for putting the pieces together. Yes, health *is* from the Latin *wholth*, which means "the pieces fit." Herein, the pieces are outlined with each being addressed with the heavenly formula. For instance, *vision* is not how you see, but how you see yourself. *Knowing* is not only perceiving, but perceiving who you are. The African proverb properly states, "It's not the name you call me, but the name I answer to." *Relationships* take us beyond loving not only because of, but loving in spite of. *Occupation* extends beyond the water cooler conversation in the work place, to selectively understanding that —

> *All the water in the world, however hard it tried,*
> *Could never ever sink a ship unless it got inside.*

Goals relate to focus, the discipline of a to-do list, a denial of what you want for what you need instead. *Accuracy* is herein, waiting for you if you have been waiting for it.

Dr. Cecil L. "Chip" Murray
The Cecil Murray Center for Community Engagement, University of Southern California

INTRODUCTION

"I want to know how to live accurately," I said to my wife one chilly winter night as we walked along Veterans Memorial Pier in Long Beach, California — something we often did during that time period. I expressed to my wife, Menzelle, both my frustration and aspiration to discover the laws that cause certain people to become successful. What I was really after was the knowledge needed to live life on its highest level in all the areas that it comprises. On a later occasion, I remember having a discussion with two of our close friends about why certain people seem to be more successful than others. During that conversation, a hunger grew in me to discover what those who demonstrate accuracy seemed to be doing right in comparison to those who weren't. As we talked, it became more apparent why a book like this is so important. There are many people searching for a better life but feel unable to attain it for one reason or another. I felt deep down in my heart that there was something that many people, including myself, were missing as it relates to obtaining the best life has to offer in relationships, financial stability, spirituality, health and the entire gamut of the human experience. The majority of us don't come from wealthy backgrounds or places of privilege. This book is for us underdogs who feel the fire of greatness within and want to get it out. One of my passions behind writing this book is to open minds to how the successful think, navigate through life and attain what they have.

As I grow in knowledge I am becoming increasingly more aware of the gaps in my own life that can hinder positive progression, as well as the places where I am "solid" that are leading to the greatness I envision. Knowledge of self, including one's strengths and weaknesses, is key to living skillfully. Then you must couple knowledge of self with the environment in which one lives in order to know the proper application for accurate lifestyle. Most importantly, a relationship with God is critical to skillful living. This writing seeks to harmonize all of these elements because they are needed to attain the best that life has to give. We live in a world where there are many obstacles and barriers to keep people from living accurately. Proof of this is seen in the divorce rates, broken homes, debt and poverty, poor health and overall dissatisfaction with life globally. There has to be a better way. One has to ask the question in light of all the devastation around us: Are we missing something? Perhaps we are not collectively living lives that are in agreement with the divine plan and we are reaping the fruit that comes from our inaccuracy.

It has been said that people perish for a lack of knowledge. Could it be that the answers that we need in order to live fulfilling and successful lives are out there, just waiting for us to discover them? I think so. I write this book from the standpoint of a fellow explorer rather than an expert. I have yet to become all that I see myself as, but one thing I am giving my life to is greater accuracy. I do not want to be another statistic that is divorced, depressed, physically and emotionally unhealthy, and generally unsatisfied with life. So if this is your pursuit as well, this is the book for you. It will not answer all of your questions, but it will spark ideas, concepts and inspiration that lead to your desire for accuracy. In this book I detail factors that I have seen contribute to my own success as well as the triumphs of other individuals, communities, ethnicities and organizations, both historically and presently.

It is my sincere hope that this book with be a valuable resource to you on your journey of increasing accuracy.

Philip "Sharp Skills" Jacobs

SECTION I

VISION AND KNOWING WHO YOU ARE

Living accurately can only be achieved when we are filled with a vision that communicates the importance of such a decision. Once we make this decision, we enter a lifelong quest of discovering who we truly are. This journey is not an easy one because it will require us to grow, perhaps in places we don't desire to because of our present level of comfort. However, in the end we will see that it was well worth the price.

CHAPTER 1

Why Live an Accurate Life

Before we get into dialogue about why living an accurate life is important, a definition is in order. At its core, an accurate life is one governed by divine authority (God) in every area of life. Many people may disagree with such a definition, but I have become convinced that there is no way for people to completely live an on-target life without following the direction of the One who created them. There are many people who reach a certain level of accuracy who don't believe in God's ultimate authority (people who I mention throughout this writing), but they have adhered to His principles in certain areas (sometimes without knowing it), thus producing the fruit of precision in their life, to a degree. For an example, think of the law of generosity. You will hear very wealthy individuals from all walks of life and faith traditions who practice this principle. This standard was created by God and is found in His ancient (yet still very relevant) text, the Bible. One of the things I often see that frustrates me is people who profess to believe in God but use that as an excuse to not become more proficient in their lives. On the flipside, I see those who are not even believers using the His laws and reaping the benefit from them. Thanks for letting me get that off my chest. Now back to my point.

There are spiritual or "invisible" laws that govern what we do see, similar to how you can't see wind but you know that it's there and see its impact. When was the last time you saw gravity? Yet, this unseen phenomena keeps you glued to the earth. And these are only natural laws! Imagine how vast and far-reaching spiritual laws are because they are not bound by time and space. The spiritual world is as real as the natural world. If this knowledge doesn't resonate with you, I challenge you to open your mind and seriously weigh what it is that I'm saying. When we violate spiritual principles, our life and planet will pay the consequences. We are seeing this play out in our environment due to our mismanagement of Earth's resources. We recognize that, without fail, we have four seasons, certain birds migrate during specific times of year, the moon goes through the same cycles every month, and the sun always rises in the east and sets in the west. There is divine protocol that has ordered the affairs of the planet as well as human life. Much of the mess humankind finds itself in is a result of not consulting with God (the Author of life) before proceeding with plans and goals. Even those who have a solid relationship with God sometimes try to move on their own.

What is the importance of living an accurate life? Why should you care about this topic? I'm glad you asked. In short, an accurate life is one that has reached its full potential and has done what it was designed to do. Just think of how great a feeling it would be as you take your last breath to know that you gave this life your best shot in all areas that were in your control. Think about how proud your Creator will be when you see Him face to face and are able to look at Him without shame as He expresses that everything He purposed for you to do in your lifetime was accomplished and in the manner in which He desired. Furthermore, accuracy enables us to leave a successful blueprint behind for our children. The excellence that we demonstrate in our lives today will impact generations to come. When a person chooses to live an accurate life, they lay a glorious foundation that their legacy (i.e. children) will be able to build upon, refine and improve. What you pioneer today will later become an easier pathway for those who follow.

> *At its core, an accurate life is one governed by divine authority in every area of life (God).*

Your reason for wanting to become more accurate in life may be different from mine, but I'm sure you deem it important nonetheless. If not, you wouldn't be reading this book. Answering the question of "why" you are pursuing something is just as important as answering the question of "what" I am pursuing. What I want you to do now is think of your motivation. Grab a notepad and jot down your thoughts right away before reading any further. Go ahead and do it! I'll be here when you get back, I promise. Ready, set, go!

Now that you have written your reasons for wanting to live a more accurate life, you must develop a precarious habit. Here it is. It is important that you keep your reasons for wanting to live an accurate life in front of you daily. If you don't, they will easily slip from your memory. The busyness of life tends to distract us if we don't fortify ourselves through repetition; we must remember what we're pursuing and why we are pursuing it. For me, images have helped tremendously in helping recall my goals. On my tablet, I have a digital image of a collage of pictures that represent what I desire for my life — a vision board, if you will. I have a picture of what I hope my family will look like, the car I want to drive, the home I want to live in, a picture of people I want to take care of financially when I am able to, and more. Whenever I open my tablet I see this and am subconsciously reminded of why I want to live a more accurate life.

The second tool I use is affirmations. I have daily affirmations that I read aloud every morning confirming who I am and what my purpose is. Here are a few of mine that you can use as a reference:

- I pursue God with my whole heart, soul, strength and mind.
- I am deeply passionate and committed to my wife, happily married and dedicated to my family.
- I am wise with my finances and have more than enough to take care of my needs and those who I am responsible for.
- I am healthy and exercise at least three times a week.

I try to read these out loud every morning before I begin my day. These declarations keep me accountable and position my goals in the forefront of my mind. There are days when I drop the ball in one of these areas, sometimes all of them. But because these affirmations are so ingrained in me, they have become a part of me. They have become my belief system. We act according to our beliefs. So when I become aware that my actions are not lining up with my core belief system, I can quickly and subconsciously change my behavior to adhere to them. As you crystallize your own reasons for wanting to live a more accurate life, I have come up with some benefits associated with doing so, to give you a framework of the possibilities.

Benefits of Accuracy

There are several benefits that come from living accurately. The four benefits that I will focus on are fulfillment, quality of life, impact and focus. These are the advantages that most impress me, but they are only a few. Feel free to ponder your own. Get creative, find pictures and affirmations that support the benefits that you come up with. Have fun with it.

> *The excellence that we demonstrate in our lives today will impact generations to come. When a person chooses to live an accurate life, they lay a glorious foundation that their legacy (i.e. children) will be able to build upon, refine and improve.*

Fulfillment

When we live life the way it was designed to be lived, we will experience fulfillment. There is an inner satisfaction that comes from being all that we were created to be. People who are fulfilled in who they are have a quiet confidence about them, which produces a strong sense of security. When you are truly fulfilled, there will be less of a need to change who you are in order to be popular because you are comfortable in your own skin. Fulfillment is a powerful element in our lives and something most people do not have.

I'm a huge Kobe Bryant fan because of his work ethic, determination and skill. When I watch him play basketball, I know that he is doing what he was designed for. I can tell that he is living accurately in this category of his life not only because he is great at the sport, but also the love for the game that he embodies. He is fulfilled in what he is doing and wouldn't rather be doing anything else. The same goes for others who find their proper lane in life and diligently remain in it. I want to paint that picture so as to give you a vision of how we should live life. We want to be accurate in every area of life that we possibly can, in the same way that our favorite sports heroes or titans of industry demonstrate accuracy in their professions. If we do this, we will find greater fulfillment and not solely in one aspect.

Finding our unique lane in life is hard enough, but our pain is compounded when we are not in sync with our divine design. You may be able to remember a job or position you held that you knew you weren't cut out for or perhaps a relationship you were trying to force that wasn't meant to be. Do you remember the frustration and dissatisfaction you felt during that time? That's the same exact feeling that inaccuracy will produce on a day-to-day basis.

On the other hand, you may be living accurately in a particular component of your life and may not be aware of it. This is actually a good thing. Hopefully we will all get to a place where accuracy is as natural as breathing. Many people have all the external trappings of success (money, cars, houses, status) but no fulfillment because they are out of alignment. Where there is a constant striving, there you will find the root of discontent. If you are living accurately, your soul will consistently be well fed, even if you go through periods of intense suffering.

One of my personal goals is to have the external components associated with success along with inner fulfillment. That's just me and the way that I'm wired. It is my desire to sacrifice neither inner nor outer fulfillment in the process of living accurately. Both of these realities should work in harmony the more accurate your life becomes.

Fulfillment frees up your mental space so that you can serve others. Unfulfilled people naturally have their minds on themselves. This is one of the worst prisons to live in. I frequently struggle with this in areas that I don't feel fulfilled. People who live skillfully and have done so for a while naturally want to give back. People who are fulfilled make the best mentors because they have crossed certain thresholds in life that have stabilized them and are successfully operating in their lane.

Quality of Life

Living accurately affects all spheres of our existence. Living according to divine design renders better relationships, financial stability, and physical and emotional health. This is not to say that those who live an accurate life will not have struggles and their fair share of hardship, but those who live skillfully will have less unnecessary bruises and setbacks. Those who live accurately don't suffer without purpose in it.

When we discover and live according to how life was meant to be lived, we reap the benefits of that choice. It is mind boggling that so many people know the good they should do and yet chose not to do it. We are all guilty of this vice. If you govern yourself and your affairs correctly, you will get the results you desire or far better. Rest assured that your choice to live accurately will have positive effects on your lifestyle, even if the results take a long time. Sometimes the results will be immediate, other times frustratingly long, but they will come nevertheless.

Shortcuts to get what we want will continually present themselves. However, those shaky foundations will come crumbling down when the pressure of success or great turmoil comes. Accuracy is the crock pot approach to success. We have to apply ourselves, narrow our foci, make wise decisions, work hard and ask for God's help each day, and soon enough we will hit our intended targets without fear of negative long-term consequences.

The rich and poor alike have 24 hours in a day to either improve or degrade their situation. A person will be provided with everything they need to get to their correct destination if they don't quit. Therefore, you and I have no excuse not to better our circumstances in every facet of life. Commitment to an accurate life will produce a better one, and the longer you work at it, the more delightful it will become. Your joy will not rest solely on your external success either; it will come from the character that developed on the inside of you as a result of your efforts.

I love reading about how Fortune 500 companies were established. Sometimes it's easy to believe that these firms came into being overnight, but the wise mind knows that isn't true. I read the story of Masura Ibuka and Akio Morita, the founders of Sony Corp. In my opinion, Sony is one of the most brilliant companies ever founded. As of this writing, it is not what it once was, but its track record is first-class. It's hard to believe that it started out as a radio repair shop and at its zenith became a multinational, billion-dollar conglomerate with more than 140,000 employees. Ibuka and Morita not only improved their own quality of life, but the lives of several thousand others.

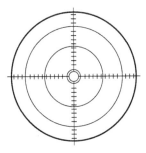

Scope of Accuracy - Sony

To this day, Sony is one of my favorite brands. Usually when I buy electronics, it will be something Sony. I wanted to dig up the reasons why Sony has made such an impression on me and millions of others.

Sony has a legacy of creating world-changing inventions such as the world's first portable TV, Japan's first transistor radio; the PlayStation brand; the world's first portable cassette player, the Sony Walkman; and countless other technological masterpieces. The Sony way of "seeking the unknown" was most embodied by the company's co-founder, Akio Morita.

While running the business, he felt strongly that a company should be more like a family than a commodity. Morita's philosophies centered on making his company prosper in the long term rather than realizing short-term gains. Sony's accuracy in the business landscape can be attributed to strong management, innovation and continuous improvement. Today, Sony is worth $28 billion.

We owe it to those who depend on us to be on target in life. Your life is the cornerstone for future generations and how well they continue to build will be based on the quality of building material you leave behind. This is not to say future generations will not be able to have a good quality of life should you get it wrong, but it makes it much more harder when the predecessor doesn't lay the appropriate foundation for tomorrow's builders. I love reading about entrepreneurs who started with nothing and died leaving a fortune for their children's children. Perhaps you may not be able to leave a wealthy estate behind for your kids, but you can start saving for their college education while they are young so that once they become of age, they don't have to worry about anything accept getting their degree. Your quality of life is not only represented by how well you live, but how well those around you are able to function.

One of the beautiful things about being connected to God is that He makes it possible not only to accumulate wealth, but to enjoy it as well. One of the challenges that I have seen few materially successful people overcome is remaining happy after success comes. To have a superb quality of life along with joy of heart is a rare feat and something that is only accomplished through wisdom that comes from the Author of life. Making the choice to live accurately gives you the opportunity to not only be successful but be happy in the process.

> *Accurate lives leave a rich legacy behind and make the journey a little easier for those who follow.*

Impact

Those who live accurately have lives that make a difference in their circles of influence. They are not just taking up space, but they contribute positive solutions to every community in which they are involved. Accurate lives leave a rich legacy behind and make the journey a little easier for those who follow. The road to leaving a significant impact is not easy but so worth it when we consider all the lives that will benefit from our good decisions.

We are still reaping the benefits of Dr. Martin Luther King Jr.'s accurate life. Doors and opportunities have been opened to every race under the sun because of him positioning himself correctly during his time on Earth. You may or may not place your faith in Jesus Christ, but the life he lived on Earth was enough to cause more than 2 billion people to profess faith in him today. When you hit your target in life, it sends ripple effects throughout time and eternity. Apple Inc. co-founder Steve Jobs will be remembered as one of the greatest inventors of all time and his contributions will continue to shape technology long after his death.

I attribute much of my framework of accuracy to my grandfather, Harold E. Phillips. He made some really good choices in his youth and because of that I have had a rich and stable foundation on which to build my future. He could have chosen to live a carefree life, but instead he chose to be faithful to one woman, work hard and live as honorably as he knew. I will forever have him as a model of what authentic accurate manhood is supposed to be. That is impact!

Think about how your life will affect those who come after you. My grandfather didn't leave me any money, but his life left me with something far greater, an honorable name. A name isn't just something on a birth certificate, but it deals with reputation and credibility. My grandfather has left a template of accuracy before me that I will always have. The greater your accuracy in life, the greater your impact will be. A life that just drifts and goes with the flow will have scattered results.

Focus

Living an accurate life allows you to set your gaze on what really matters. Those who live skillfully are not caught up in petty events. Accuracy gives us insight into what we are responsible for so that we do not become encumbered by that which we are not. People who are focused accomplish more, in lesser time and with greater result.

In his book *The Millionaire Real Estate Investor*, real estate mogul Gary Keller stated, "Focus is the key to success, more than effort, experience, or even natural ability. Look at the highest achievers in any field and you'll discover that they have powerful focus. Just as important, you'll learn that they focus on the right things: the handful of truly important issues that make the biggest difference."

Accuracy allows us to cut through to the heart of things and make decisions based on the root issues instead of the fluff. Many people make their choices on superfluous information and not on what really matters. How much difference do you think it would make in your life if you executed your movements according to information that was true? Warren Buffet, arguably one of the world's most successful investors, is known to make his investment decisions not based on the opinions of popular media or those of the market, but on annual reports (which he voraciously studies) and the true valuation of a company. To take it even further, Buffet will not invest in a business or industry that he doesn't understand.

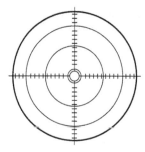

Scope of Accuracy – Warren Buffet

Many people are not aware that one of the world's wealthiest people, Warren Buffet, is from Omaha, Nebraska. This is why he is dubbed "The Oracle of Omaha." The only reason I probably know this is because I lived in Omaha for three years when I was in high school. This financial giant is very down-to-earth, still living in his first home that he bought in the 1950s.

Buffet only makes his investment decisions based on the soundest information possible. No wonder his net worth (as of this writing) is in excess of $50 billion, according to Forbes. Buffet has made some bad investment moves in his career, but his overall accurate methodology allows him to succeed despite the losses he has taken. He focuses on the key information, makes the most accurate maneuver and comes out on top. Where a person places their focus determines where they will end up. Accuracy demands that you place your attention on what matters and leads to the desired result.

This is by no means an exhaustive list of the benefits that stem from an accurate life. Perhaps you can take some time now and write down some other benefits that you feel accompany skillful living. It is imperative that more and more people choose to live accurately.

Doing Life Incorrectly

As a society we've become skillful at doing life incorrectly and generations to come will have to absorb those costs. You and I have the opportunity to set a new standard and, hopefully, divert some of the catastrophic events that will be brought about in the near future. It is not the responsibility of government and the educational system to teach us how to live according to the rules that properly govern humankind. It will take those who are willing to develop new habits and thought processes that go against the grain of conventional wisdom to cause significant transformation. Accurate minds need to be cultivated and then planted in arts and entertainment, business, government, education, health care, media and religion.

It's so disheartening to see that if something, even a lie, is touted as truth for long enough, the majority of people will accept it. We must be proactive in checking the information we regard as truth, and this must be done on a regular basis. We all have to evaluate ourselves from time to time in order to recognize what deceptions we may have bought into. I've even noticed that many people in the faith community take what a minister says as law, even if it is incorrect and unbiblical. Or perhaps we accept something as truth because our mother or father said it was such. One must be careful to keep the baby but throw out the dirty bath water when it comes to the information we consume.

> *Accuracy allows us to cut through to the heart of things and make decisions based on the root issues instead of the fluff.*

Marketing departments at large companies count on our inability to stop and check every message we receive through media and as result, we give in (often subconsciously) to messages that are incongruent with accurate lifestyle. For example, one category this is seen in is food. Throughout the past several decades, people have been mentally conditioned to eat what is good to them rather than what is good for them. The majority of us have fallen for this falsehood, especially me. We can't place all of the blame on the strategic marketing ploys of food service companies because much of what happens to us is based on the poor choices that we make. But these marketers do a good job of encouraging us to make the wrong ones. Once we saturate our minds and taste buds with what we deem is "good," we no longer have a desire to eat what is truly good for us.

Here's somewhat of a funny story to drive home what I'm talking about. I remember one time my wife bought organic chicken from the grocery store and she didn't tell me that's what it was. I just assumed that it was the regular chicken we always ate. When she served dinner, she noticed that I wasn't eating it. "What's wrong with the food?" she asked, concerned. I reluctantly had to tell her that the chicken was not appetizing to me. When she told me it was organic chicken, I thought to myself, "I've become so accustomed to the conventional type that my taste buds required that to be satisfied."

It is easy to target and vilify poor financial and relational management skills, but we often overlook that poor consumption of food is something to be on guard against as well. Once we fill our bodies with "delicious poison" we must then take costly "medicated poisons" to reduce the delicious poison's effect. But, of course, the medicated poison has its terrible side effects on both our health and pocketbooks. Accurate lifestyle will encourage eating and exercising habits that promote longevity and good physical mobility. The disclaimer I will continue to give throughout this book is that by no means have I achieved the complete accuracy I discuss, but am in hot pursuit of it, as are you.

Here is another example of so-called conventional wisdom that is not in alignment with accurate lifestyle. Debt is seen as something that is required in our modern society. It's almost as if you are from another planet if you mention that you don't have any debt or some other financial fiasco pervading your life. Again, people buy into a false belief system that keeps them captive and unable to move as they should. Budgeting and living below ones means are not the norm for many people. According to the Federal Reserve's G.19 on consumer credit, U.S. consumer debt was $2.43 trillion as of May 2011. Now let's compare apples to apples. According to the Bureau of Business and Economic Research, total U.S. personal income was $12.3 billion in 2010. That is a $2.42 trillion deficit. If that isn't inaccurate money management to you, I don't know what is.

Inaccuracy is accepted as the norm. The masses allow themselves, sometimes unknowingly, to be brainwashed and herded into a direction leading to ruin. I don't know about you, but I don't want to live a self-destructive lifestyle just because it is regarded as normal. I'm going to fight with everything in me to make sure that I and those who I am responsible for are able to live life well and master it. You owe it to those you love to make correct decisions and model an on-target lifestyle. I should probably add that an accurate life doesn't mean a perfect life. We humans have flaws. There is no way around it. The principle of accuracy is to align oneself with divine protocol. It is a process of constant discovery and rediscovery of one's driving lane in life, and the best way to move in it during their lifetime.

I once heard someone say that the grave is the richest place on earth. There you will find books that were never written, degrees never obtained, businesses never started, society-altering relationships never formed, inventions never created, and $2 trillion ideas never implemented. I wonder how much of this reality stems from those who have died that never moved into a place of accuracy; I'm willing to bet almost all. Accuracy will allow us to produce what we were designed to create. We all have a niche to occupy that will make the world a little better. Just imagine an entire family, community, city or nation dedicated to being on target. What if that nation's government handled its affairs in a way that aligned with correct principles? Even imagining such a thing is farfetched. Yet, people like you may move into a place of political prominence, and because you have cultivated an accurate life beforehand, you will automatically take that into your position. You would be able to influence others to desire and employ accuracy. That's exactly how this thing will spread.

An accurate husband will seek ways to enhance his marriage and family experience. He will develop strong bonds with his spouse and children according to their "love language." An inaccurate husband will govern his home sloppily and not take the time to understand who his spouse and children are and what their needs are. We will see stronger families that are able to weather oppressive influences that are eroding the family structure once members of the home make it an ambition to become more accurate.

A Lesson Learned

I remember a time when I was in college taking a class on strategic business. A passing course grade was based on a group project, a business strategy game that we had to play against other groups in the class. As a group, we were a shoe company competing against others for better market share, return on equity, positive credit rating, image rating and stock prices. Before we started the game, our instructor told us that the key to success in this game was reading the 90-page manual in its entirety and that if we didn't it would only be a matter of time before a group failed. Well guess what, our group, including myself, did not take the time to read the manual and I passed that class by the skin of my teeth. There was key information that we needed in order to be successful. Our group got into a lot of arguments and disputes, which probably could have been avoided if we had all taken the time to learn how to play. Many of the decisions we made were based on guess work or secondhand information from other groups, who were failing too, might I add. The successful groups weren't going to give up their strategies as easy. We watched other teams conquer us with glee as their make-believe stock prices rose above ours at an astronomical rate. They patted each other on the back and gave each other high fives as they presented their weekly numbers to the instructor, who congratulated them in front of us. This did not feel good at all. I learned a valuable lesson in that class. If there are rules out there that give me a better shot at success, then I will not neglect them.

I don't want to make life sound trivial, but much of our existence is similar to a strategic game simulation. God reveals the information necessary to master life and come out on top. In order to truly live skillfully, we have to live according to correct principles. Harmful information is in abundance, much like the bad advice that we received from the other failing groups in my strategic business class. We followed their advice blindly because we didn't know the rules that led to success. So it will take a good deal of effort to obtain and understand the correct information and put it into practice. Otherwise, we will succumb to the overwhelming amount of misinformation swirling around us. The good news is that the correct information is readily available. It's up to you and me to find that information though. I once read, "It is God's privilege to conceal things and the king's privilege to discover them" (Proverbs 25:2, New Living Translation). The king or queen in you has the esteemed purpose of uncovering the hidden treasures of wisdom in day-to-day life. What an honor! There are nuggets of wisdom for skillful living all around us that many don't take advantage of.

It makes life much more interesting when you engage in it as a treasure hunt. So many of us only settle for sand rather than the buried treasure. Choosing to live an accurate life is much like a treasure hunt, yet people are deciding to accept a life of mediocrity, which is the highway to an overly critical and cynical attitude. It's no wonder people have such a hard time cheering for someone who is garnering success and improving their situation. People who decide to live accurately are discovering buried treasure and that puts pressure on those who decide to only dig in the sand. We all must come to terms with our sand digging when someone close to home strikes gold. The reality sets in that there is potential that is being discovered and utilized by some and not others. It is easier to support others and cheer them on in their success when we become more accurate and accomplish success in our own spheres of responsibility.

Supporting Others

Our human flaws prevent us from being supportive of others who are progressing in their potential when we are not doing the same. Therefore, another major benefit connected to living accurately is that you will genuinely encourage others who are living accurately as well, without jealousy or envy. It is my sincere belief that when people are busy and thriving in their lane, they will not have the time or desire to knock someone else for their achievements. If you are like me, you know one of the worst feelings to have in the heart is envy. Those who are not uncomfortable feeling that way have entertained that emotion too long and need to work on discarding it for their own good.

By studying others who have moved into a place of prominence that you would like to mirror, you increase your chances of doing the same.

Those who decide to pursue and find their correct place in life inadvertently put pressure on those who are unwilling to do the same. People who are not in their proper lane are prone to criticize others who are. I vacillate between both realities at times. When we find ourselves slacking off in a certain area and experience failure as a result, we are more prone to badmouth others who are advancing. However, when we begin to apply ourselves and are productive within our own spheres of influence, we will be able to wholeheartedly cheer others on who are doing the same. No one will ever be perfect in this area though; it's just the result of being an imperfect human.

Developing the ongoing habit of precise execution produces a greater appreciation for others who are doing the same. One who remains in a state of veracity will applaud achievers around them because they recognize how hard it is. When you understand someone's journey, it makes it easier to identify with them and this establishes a greater level of camaraderie. Individuals with skillful lives are secure in who they are and don't see their counterparts as a threat. Rather, it is heartening to see that you are not alone.

A hardworking businessperson with a Lamborghini probably isn't disturbed by another professional with a Ferrari. They realize that they have something in common and probably share similar stories on how they came to acquire such exquisite vehicles. On the flipside, it is more probable that a slouch (even a hardworking person) with a Pinto would more than likely envy such people. One thing I made up in my mind to do a while ago was to use others' accomplishments as fuel for my own drive. Instead of being upset with a guy who pulls up in a Bentley alongside my bucket at a stoplight, I admire them (in my head of course) and say that I can have the same. Should I ever make up in my mind that I will no longer pursue a life of accuracy, I will then drift into discontentment when I come across those who are progressing. The cars and money to acquire aren't the point I'm trying to get across here. Whether you have a nice vehicle or not is not important. The character that allows us to sincerely support the good happening in other people's lives is a sign of accuracy. When you know that you are in progress and are getting closer to your destination, there is an appreciation for the next person who may be a little further along in their journey.

The more time we spend worried about another person's journey, the less time we will have to give thought to your own. I find that I am most productive and content when I concentrate on where I am headed as oppose to someone else. I'm then able to lend support to others with a genuine heart. Many of us have experienced seasons where we poured everything we had into another person's vision and received very little or nothing at all in return. Afterward, we felt the disappointment of not making any real progress in our personal journey. Bitterness, jealousy and contempt can soon grow in our hearts if we are not careful. We have to learn how to simultaneously further our efforts while assisting others with theirs. It is a balancing act of doing what we are put on earth to accomplish and also give others the push that they need in order to do the same.

We are all wired to be productive. Be we cannot be productive when we spend all of our time in another person's domain. Now this isn't to say that there aren't periods where you are positioned to promote and push someone further only. Many times we have to go through a phase like this to develop greater character, experience and skill in our own endeavors. We should all be a part of something larger than ourselves. We should look at our personal endeavors as rivers and lakes that connect to a vast ocean. There are certain periods of time when we are to lend ourselves to another river and other times when we must focus on our individual streams. We should always keep our eyes on the greater ocean though. OK, enough with the philosophical water talk. Let's move on.

To counter the all-too-common human emotions of jealousy and envy, we must become preoccupied with fine tuning our own lives. We have to learn to appreciate and even emulate those we admire and who have done what we one day hope to accomplish as well. One habit that I have developed throughout the years is making people who I look up to my mentors, even if I have never met or spoken with them. They mentor me through their books, audio programs, website content and other communication methods. I observe their actions and how they interact with others. There are even some people that I consider peers that mentor me in certain areas of life, sometimes without them knowing. Taking this approach will allow us to learn and be happy for their success. Their successful model provides the frame of reference necessary for our learning curve to be reduced. If they were unsuccessful, no one would be better off because there would be no wealth of knowledge to share.

Author of *The Millionaire Mind*, Thomas J. Stanley, Ph.D., introduced me to a powerful idea. I'm not sure if he intended to become wealthy as a result of studying the wealthy; nonetheless, a light bulb went off in my head about a key element that produces accuracy in any endeavor. By studying others who have moved into a place of prominence that you would like to mirror, you increase your chances of doing the same. One of the reasons I wrote this book was to dive deeper into the world of the mind of people who demonstrate precision so I can understand how they think and incorporate what they do in my life. Therefore, I don't spend my time being upset that they are making strides, but I am able to support them and legitimately be happy for their success.

I realize that the success of others is my success as well to a certain degree. If there was no one to take the bumps and bruises spread across the road of accuracy, we would have it that much harder. We would have to find that route ourselves without a forerunner's wisdom to help guide us along the way.

The Life of Accuracy Is the Life That Matters

Imagine that you bought two chairs for your home. Your purpose for getting these chairs is to accommodate guests when they come to your home for afternoon tea. You've built quite the following at your tea parties and need more seats. One of the chairs that you bought is elegant and regal, built with gold and plush burgundy velvet cushions. You paid a whopping $1,000 for this grandiose butt rest! Now the other chair that you bought is a plain-old fold-out with plastic cushions that you bought for $30. When guests come over, you discover that the $1,000 throne has a major problem; it collapses when anyone sits in it. It can't hold the weight of even a newborn baby without falling apart. What's worse, this problem cannot be fixed. The chair is irreparable. Yet the $30 chair is much sturdier and does the job. It can even accommodate your 400-pound aunt, Beulah. Which chair would you consider more valuable, as it relates to serving the purpose for which you purchased it? I think you get where I'm going with this.

Though the $30 chair was less expensive than the gaudy throne you also purchased, it is worth more to you in the long run because it serves its purpose. That chair is the one that makes the most difference at your parties. The $1,000 chair is ineffective and you would probably be ashamed to share how much you paid for it, if someone were to ask. When you get to the point of being definite in your purpose, your contributions become more valuable than those of others who chose not to be. Don't misunderstand what I am saying: Every human life is valuable and no one should act as if they are better than anybody else. The point I'm making is that a person who has an accurate life is worth more, in terms of effectiveness, than someone just wandering around aimlessly. There are many who go through life playing the part of accuracy (i.e. that they have it all together) but habitually miss the mark. They work hard at appearances, much like the expensive chair, but they have no substance.

Here is another example of what I mean. Two employees get hired by the same company on the same day. They are equals in rank in the company. Employee A keeps a low profile, works diligently and produces results that benefit the company, while Employee B lollygags and pretends to be productive when in front of the boss, yet the majority of the time he is wasting the employer's dime. By the company's standards, Employee A is by far the more valuable employee. Employee A is serving the purpose for why they were hired, which is to add value to the company. Employee B appears to be hitting the mark, but it will only be a matter of time before he is entangled in his false advertisement. The company will soon find out and Employee B will either be fired or disciplined, while Employee A gets a pat on the back and promotion eventually.

On an even larger scale, we see cases where greater society prefers to be the expensive chair or Employee B. A lot of what we see, hear and read has no value at all. It doesn't truly matter. Most of it will neutralize our effectiveness and hinder our divine design. Accurate minds chose to rise above the clouds of nonsense that hover over us. The many people that remain under these clouds think their lives are heading in the right direction when they're not. I'm reminded of a proverb concerning this: "There is a way that appears to be right, but in the end it leads to death" (Proverbs 14:12, New International Version). The masses believe they are on the right track as long as they go to work, pay their bills, spend time with family, impress their peers and even attend church occasionally. All of these are great things (and I practice them), but you can do all this and still miss the intended mark for your life. Sadly, many people go to the grave without having the impact they were designed to have. Their lives end up not mattering in the grand scheme of things. You and I have to fight against the mentality that says, "I'm OK if I just cover the basics of life," or the self-deception that says, "I'm going somewhere," when we're really stagnant. Every individual has a complexity about themselves that is meant to be discovered, refined and shaped into something phenomenal. We do ourselves and the world we live in a great disservice if we don't realize all of who we are meant to be and express it.

Steve Jobs, heralded as one of the greatest inventors of all time realized that he was on to something with his technology company, Apple. He was convinced that he could change the world and technology was the medium he would use to accomplish that feat. Jobs persuaded John Sculley, who at the time was president of Pepsi Co., to leave his executive position to come run Apple with him. He is famous for saying to the reluctant at the time Sculley, "Do you want to sell sugared water for the rest of your life or do you want to change the world?" That statement captures the essence of what I want to convey. Sure, you could take the comfortable route, sell sugared water and appease the status quo. Or you could be a part of history and remembered for being a part of something great, even if it's on a small scale. Greatness doesn't always mean big, and big doesn't always mean great. There are some people we will never hear of who left an indelible mark on human affairs, but Heaven knows them well.

> *There is a specific crowd you were made to reach. The experiences, background and characteristics you have are for that special group of people.*

Whenever you are tempted to be mediocre, follow the lemmings and get off track, go make yourself a cup of nice cold sugar water. Then ask yourself, "Is this all that I am worth?" OK, so you probably won't do that, but you get the picture.

People who live skillful lives are people who matter. They become great anchors for others in their surroundings and act as conduits that create opportunities to advance for future generations. Those who are accurate understand their purpose and flourish in it. A life that matters is a life that makes the space it occupies better. There is a weight and authority that accompanies individuals who are fulfilling their function. They are able to command their environments because they have earned the respect necessary to do so. This authority comes from the sacrifices they make to be who they are. Walking the path of correctly defined direction is narrow and few are willing to travel on it. This path is one of greatness that will be remembered by future generations. Accurate sojourners are in demand in these days, and the world at large is beginning to sense the need for these types of people. If you stay in your lane and continue to hone who you are, others will take note and follow.

The people we are meant to influence will be drawn to us when we perform our proper function in life. There is no need to go chasing after notoriety when we stand in our designated position. It is a common temptation to adjust who we are to gain outside acceptance. I have learned not to try to be something I'm not just to gain the approval of others. Other people that have had sustainable success knew they had to be true to who they were. When we are not true to ourselves, we get out of sync and lose credibility with the people we are supposed to influence. You have to be authentic when you exercise your purpose. Don't lose one and attempt to gain the other — they both work in tandem. There is a specific crowd you were made to reach. The experiences, background and characteristics you have are for that special group of people. The challenge is to skillfully be you.

A life that matters is one that is coveted by all but refused by many. People fold to the pressure of a world system that seeks to neuter and suppress their potency. Fear is a powerful foe that grips our minds and convinces us to play it safe so we don't suffer loss. Accurate persons weigh the costs of playing it safe and know that, in the long run, that fee is much higher than paying the price of fulfilling their purpose.

One of my favorite movies is *Braveheart*. There is a scene in the movie where William Wallace, portrayed by Mel Gibson, addresses the frightened Scottish army who were arguing with each other about whether to fight the oppressive king of England or tuck tail and run. Wallace inspired them by saying that they would live if they ran home and didn't fight, but they would regret it when they were old. They would long for the opportunity again to stand on that battlefield and regret that they didn't fight when they had the chance. Everyone in their heart of hearts wants to have a life that makes a difference, but many will end up being paralyzed by fear and never acting on what is in their heart. They will one day wake up full of regret because they didn't do what was necessary during their window of opportunity.

Determine in your mind to be accurate, ultimately living a life that makes a difference and serves its God-given purpose. Anything else will result in frustration. Spend the time most would use to just look the part (the fancy chair) and use that to actually be the part (less expensive but more useful chair). If you can both look the part and be the part, then do it. But the most important thing is to actually have a life of value, and that does not consist of mere appearance.

I hope this chapter has given you insight as to why accuracy is so important and the benefits of it. There's a great need, now more than ever, for people to step up to the plate and live accurate lives for the sake of their families, communities and nations. We cannot afford any more misdirection, especially by those who claim to know the answers. As we have uncovered, there are several pluses associated with the accurate life. I encourage you to revisit this section of the book when inspiration is needed to stay on track.

Application of Accuracy:

- Keep your reasons for wanting to be accurate in front of you daily (e.g. collage, pictures, phrases).
- Use affirmations to express who you are and what your purpose is.
- Remind yourself that accuracy can produce a better quality of life, increase your impact, hone your focus and bring inner fulfillment.

CHAPTER 2

Vision

Vision is probably the most important quality one can possess as it relates to living accurately. Vision provides us with the motivation needed to stay the course, even when it's difficult. You don't have to be a visionary (which is more so a personality trait) to have a vision, but everyone should have one for where they are headed. If you don't, don't worry. A true vision cannot be forced. It will come at the right time for you.

Everything starts from an idea, which is another word I use to describe vision. Everything we see worth noting in this life came from someone's foresight of what could be. Vision is a powerful quality that allows you to work and live from the unrealized possibilities within and around you. So many people imprison themselves because they operate based off of what their current limitations are. If you want to model an accurate lifestyle, you must decide to uproot your thinking from the soil of focusing solely on your current station in life and move it to who your vision says you can be. This is not to say that we shouldn't keep a firm grasp on reality; we must balance the here and now with what can be eventually.

What Do You Envision?

We should think of vision as a seed planted deep within us. It is our job to nurture it in order for it to grow (as far as it depends on us). We also have to guard what we allow into our gardens because those outside elements will greatly impact these seeds. Unfortunately, we can't control what goes on around us. Sometimes we are placed in environments and conditions that we didn't choose for ourselves. It can be tricky to navigate around this, but it is still your responsibility (ultimately) to do everything in your power to make sure you bring to fruition the vision entrusted to you.

What you envision is an important question to answer because it ultimately decides which direction you will take. What we see is often what we believe is possible. If you only see and expect a life of poverty, you are more likely to stay in a cycle of perpetual debt, poor spending habits and bad financial choices. Sadly, this is the case for many, even though they may not realize it. Negative vision can be so entrenched in people that it takes substantial time and effort for correct vision to be built within them. Buried in each individual is the awareness of who they are meant to be, but life and circumstances have a way of blurring that reality and making it appear unattainable. We can even see the effects that stem from lack of vision in society as a whole. Lack of vision is prevalent in several communities and groups, and this causes those within them to be low-level achievers, complacent and depressed.

I would like to interject here that, on the other hand, there are also people who were raised to believe that their visions were very achievable. My mother raised me to believe that I could be anything that I desired, which is why I have a strong inclination to take risks and be entrepreneurial. The values she instilled in me at a very young age have caused me to view life through a larger scope. Even when I went through a destructive phase that contradicted the value system built inside me, those same seeds still governed what I thought possible. Some people get ahead in life simply because they had a vision that they chose to pursue with all of their strength. Ninety percent of what they do is tied to it and they are quick to eliminate anything that detracts from it.

When there is poor inner vision built within someone, the value that they place on life will be reduced. It is easier to put harmful chemicals in the body, engage in dangerous sexual activity, and give little thought to the welfare of yourself and others when vision is restricted. People will value the wrong things and allow damaging philosophies to govern their lives when they can't see themselves for who they were created to be. We all can fall prey to limited vision for various reasons. The goal is to break this negative pattern of thinking and operate from a greater visual horizon.

Sometimes individuals have a clear vision of who they are but their environment contradicts what they see. When the environment (a message in and of itself) is reinforced by other negative messages on a consistent enough basis, then an individual is prone to take their reality as truth over their positive internal vision. On the other hand, even if someone maintains a positive vision of themselves, their inaccurate perspective can cause self-deception that leads them to believe that the positive destination they see in their mind will fall into their lap. I like to call this the "everything will work out eventually" syndrome. They believe that just because they see a positive outcome in their mind that actions don't have to accompany their faith for it to actually happen. So many people find that eventually never comes. When you live your life aimlessly, vision turns into fantasy.

I've been on both sides of this coin. Personally, I have had to learn (and continue to learn) that even though sometimes reality contradicts my vision, I will eventually see it blossom if I stay on the path of accuracy. A foreman has a blueprint (vision), but he has to build (work) according to those plans (accuracy) to construct something. Vision enables us to sacrifice short-term comfort for the long-term benefit of its realization. I understand why I do what I do; it is tied to my destiny. We can't let discouragement of what we see now cause us to make decisions that will keep us from capturing what is promised. Your vision is a promise and it is the personal incentive used to keep you and I focused on becoming more accurate. Vision drives us to add things to our lives that help us obtain the good that lies ahead. There are behavioral patterns and thought processes that have to be discarded before we are permitted to move closer to our visions. Once those are discarded, new thought processes and patterns have to become established.

Coming to the knowledge that the realization of a vision doesn't just fall out of the sky did not happen overnight for me. A vision coming to fruition always works together with making difficult (yet necessary) choices, character development and hard work. As I just mentioned, the skyscrapers that we see didn't just appear. There was a blueprint, permits were pulled, materials were purchased, construction crews were assembled, money was raised, heavy equipment utilized and a host of other elements came into play to build these magnificent structures.

The same is true for you and I — we have magnificent structures and systems on the inside of us that want to get out. If truth be told, much of the frustration people feel stems from not having the power (ability) or understanding (know-how) to produce what they envision. I'm willing to bet that the visions many people have overwhelm them when they try to consider how they will be accomplished. What do most people do as a result of this? They tend to go into autopilot, become complacent, and sweep their vision under the rug. The human mind has a mechanism that protects us from sensory overload, which is the reason why we all have prejudgments. Instead of wrestling with how to make our vision a reality, we put it somewhere deep within a secret room in our minds and go on with our normal life. This protection from the unfathomable (in our current state of mind and being) can also be a great limitation for us if we don't recognize when it is in operation. We are all tempted to just go into maintenance mode instead of striving to get in line with our larger vision. There are others who passionately pursue their vision and get so worn out from failed attempts that they give up and settle for something else of far lesser value. A God-given vision takes a long time to become a reality. There is always a journey. The journey is what molds us into who we must become to handle the responsibility that comes with the vision. And that journey can be overwhelming.

Why Does Your Vision Overwhelm You?

There are three main reasons why vision can overwhelm us. The first reason is that we can't always see how we will accomplish it with our current resources. And they're not just limited to finances. When we weigh our vision in light of what our current situation is, it looks impossible. The problem lies in us trying to figure things out with our own wisdom and limited knowledge. The man who is truly wise knows that he doesn't hold all of the answers. Sure you're gifted, talented and popular, but in the face of accomplishing a gigantic vision, those things (alone) don't stand a chance.

The truth is, we can't accomplish our vision as who we are right now and solely by ourselves. I've seen many people make the mistake of trying to tackle their vision as soon as it popped into their head. I've even personally committed this blunder several times. As a result, their businesses and endeavors failed miserably. There is a process that we all must go through before we transform our

> *There is a process that we all must go through before we transform our vision from concept to reality. For one, our character needs to be solid enough to handle the success and responsibility that comes with our future position.*

vision from concept to reality. For one, our character needs to be solid enough to handle the success and responsibility that comes with our future position. David, the great biblical figure, was designated as the future king of Israel when he was a boy and did not step into that reality until he was in his thirties. Throughout that period of time, he was almost killed by Saul (the current king), killed a giant warrior (Goliath), fought wars and became a fugitive on the run for his life. He was shaped and prepared for his kingship so that he would not get into office and be destroyed by the weight of his responsibility. God wanted to keep tabs on him (as any good parent does) in order to protect him from himself when he acquired more power. He had to be humbled so that he would properly handle his influence. Even with all that he went through, the power still managed to go to his head, causing judgment lapses that almost cost him his kingdom. We should be aware of the human condition in all of us that can cause us to blow our future, even when we go through extensive preparation (trials and suffering) and come out of it. So how much more is someone likely to screw up their vision if their character isn't well developed? The answer is, very likely. We see in the press time after time people who are well known falling from grace in one way or another. Many times, this is due to there being secret areas in our lives that go unchecked and lack of accountability while influence was small. Since those places were not matured before their vision was realized, they suffered great consequences when it was. Count it as a gift if you have to go through a major growth phase before you move to a higher station in life. You will have a fighting chance to not fall into the traps that the "high life" conceals. Jim Graff hit the nail right on the head in his book, *A Significant Life*, when he stated that leaders and people with great influence live on dangerous emotional levels which make them more prone to making devastating mistakes. Therefore, they have to find a way to stay grounded.

Aside from character, skill level has to increase to a degree that matches our vision. You will not, for example, become a millionaire real estate investor overnight. There are those rare cases when people get boosted to a greater platform in a fairly short amount of time (I have experienced this myself), but life has a way of slowing us down if we move too fast. There comes a point in time where we all have to earn the bread we eat and pay the cost to do what we do. There are seasons that we just can't fast forward through. We will have to put forth the required work and sacrifice to see a vision come to pass. If you want to be accurate, a time will come when you will have to make the choice to develop a particular set of skills during an extended period of time that will enable you to accomplish your vision. A higher skill level will produce greater confidence, which will make what was a challenging vision more attainable.

David more than likely had a hard time reconciling his current reality with his future status. He was a lowly shepherd and the youngest of his brothers. Those two facts alone contradicted a vision of future kingship. David had to embark on a long and painful journey toward that vision and trust that God would get him there, despite the obstacles along the way. I can imagine that transitioning from a shepherd to a king was an overwhelming thought. A more modern context would probably be someone in poverty being told that they will one day be the president of the United States. Could you imagine? One minute you're trying to figure out how to come up with gas money, and the next minute you're making decisions as the leader of the free world. There is a certain mindset one must have in order to be a president. Someone phasing out of poverty and into the White House probably wouldn't do very well in that office if they were just thrown into it without extensive preparation. The same is true for us in our spheres of influence; we must first be developed and then deployed into these new territories to have the best chance at succeeding.

The fact is, we will not be who we are today when we are living out our vision. God is not going to entrust us with his best until we first become the best. Best doesn't mean perfect. In this sense of the word, it pertains to the maturity, heart position and integrity levels needed to properly handle greater responsibility. He loves you and me too much to let his blessing destroy us. Your vision is a blessing — treat it as such. We all have to be stretched to manage the greater positions we will occupy. I have noticed that the larger things that I've accomplished and/or been entrusted with came after significant periods of mental and spiritual growth. There are often seasons of pain, suffering and loss before substantial gain comes. We learn more in periods of tribulation than we do in times of ease. Things that were once imposing feats became more attainable (and believable) the more I grew as a person. I was ready to handle these great milestones once my priorities shifted and I understood the true purpose behind why I was to achieve them. Our vision is always for a greater purpose than what we currently know at the time. If we move immediately into what we envision, we will not have had the right mindset when it becomes tangible. Dependence upon God has to become the cornerstone in our understanding before we are permitted to start building. I've learned to not get too happy with the large visions that I hold because I know there is a sobering (and sometimes very painful) training process attached to them. My outlook is not one of "doom or gloom," but I now understand that there will be some painful personal changes that need to take place along the journey. We have to grow into our visions, and growth is never an easy process.

The second reason why people become overwhelmed with their vision is that they don't see the necessary role community plays in it. The western cultural mindset of individualism is so prevalent that we often try to figure out how we can become great on our own. Anything great and that has lasting impact will not and cannot be accomplished alone. Though Dr. Martin Luther King Jr. was the main figurehead of the Civil Rights Movement, it was the people associated with it that gave it its strongest momentum. King had a vision, but that vision would've never materialized if he tried to be the lone ranger. His famous "I Have a Dream" speech would have remained just that.

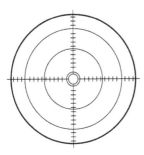

Scope of Accuracy – Dr. Martin Luther King Jr.

Martin Luther King Jr. has become the undisputed icon of the Civil Rights Movement. He demonstrated intense bravery and perseverance in the face of staunch opposition from the U.S. government, hate groups and even his own peers in the Christian ministry. Somehow, he was able to overcome his fears and insecurities and lead a nation to realize the dream of equality and brotherhood amongst all people regardless of their race.

A rebel of sorts, King went against his father's wishes of joining the black Atlanta aristocracy and instead joined forces with the Freedom Riders, a group of radical college students who fought against segregation. King decided against living the easy life of the inaccurate status quo that many of his peers and elders advocated. Although King's passion and fervor for equality and denouncement of the Vietnam War led his life to be claimed in an assassination, the accuracy he demonstrated in his lifetime continues to echo in modern reality.

There is a strength found in teams that can never be had by just one individual acting alone, no matter how talented they are. You will find that the greatest leaders aren't necessarily always the smartest, most gifted or even the most influential, but they are the best team builders. When there is a group of people on the same page and sharing the load, it makes the vision much more feasible. The feeling of being overwhelmed comes when we are wearing too many hats. We are made to be interdependent; there is no way around it. Even if you have an independent personality, you will eventually come to appreciate that you need others in order to accomplish your vision.

Contrary to what we are taught, there is no such thing as a self-made person. Many so-called gurus would like to lead us to believe that they did it all on their own. While their drive, motivation and ambition caused them to follow through on their vision, they never would have reached the finish line without the help of others along the way. The most successful people are those who embrace the help of others. Furthermore, they know what skills they lack and utilize the strengths of others where they are deficient. I sincerely believe that the greatest visionaries are those that fulfill the individual visions of those on their team. King had a vision that resonated in the hearts and minds of those around him. They had the same vision; he was just the one who could articulate it. King unlocked the potential contained in the hearts of his followers. You may or may not have ever experienced this, but I've been a part of visions that were given to other leaders that had my individual vision as a component within theirs. One of the reasons I was able to follow them wholeheartedly is because I had buy-in. I saw my place within their overall vision and so I championed it

> *Never underestimate the power of community. The people that thrive are the ones that have a strong sense of unity and interconnectedness.*

as my own, because it was. This brings me to another point: We should always be a part of a vision that is bigger than our own and should include others who find their place in our vision.

A vision is never meant to be accomplished alone. The more like-minded (not necessarily similar) people who we surround ourselves with will make what we envision come to pass. Never underestimate the power of community. The people who thrive are the ones who have a strong sense of unity and interconnectedness. They share the same values and goals, and see further than just individual success. The power lies in promoting (in sincerity, not for manipulation) a vision that others buy into as well. This requires a great deal of maturity, unselfishness and, in some cases, training because we have to be willing to sacrifice our egos and allow others to take ownership of what we see. A piece of what you see may be someone else's entire vision and life's purpose.

Individualism is a weakness that masks itself as self-sufficient power. There is nothing wrong about being an individual (which is what makes you unique), but individualism, on the other hand, promotes self-destructive isolation. We are limited to solely realizing only our "personal" best when we operate in an individualistic paradigm. We can do things beyond our wildest dreams when we tap into the potential of a team. A great team will always be better than a superstar player.

The third reason why vision overwhelms us is that we try to bring it to fruition without God's help. We easily forget that God has assigned a purpose to each one of us. He has placed desires, ambitions, gifts and talents within us. Things get messy when we try to go after a God-given vision without His direction. We end up with needless bumps and bruises when we don't walk in step with God.

I find that I have the most confidence when I have spent adequate time in God's presence through prayer, meditation and worship. The days that I don't do this, I am lost. The visions God created us to produce are only able to come about with His help. Some chose to get help from some other spiritual sources to arrive at the platform they seek. They may make it to the level they dream of, but much trouble is attached to it. Conversely, God will take us through some painful character-building sessions along the way, but once we make it to our designated places we will be thankful for it.

God gives us visions that we absolutely cannot produce on our own. He allows us to be the visionary, but it is ultimately Him who will enable us to see it through. What we produce in this life should be done on God's terms. If we do this, we will be examples of accuracy to those around us. Don't fall into the trap of trying to make your vision tangible without God's help. Part of the reason we see high divorce rates, poor health and depression among society's successful is that somewhere along the way, they left God behind. That's not to say that those who have a true relationship with God will not (and do not) face the same problems. However, He gives us the wherewithal to survive and get to our destination despite them.

Trusting in God does not assuage the fact that we will have to work hard to make our vision a reality. There are many who think that faith alone will get them to where they want to be. This couldn't be further from the truth. One has to combine faith in God with a strong work ethic. God will not do what is in our power to do; He takes over once we've done everything that he has instructed us to do. Our involvement in the process of accomplishing our vision makes us appreciate it more once we obtain it. People have a tendency not to value things as much when they get it without building any sweat equity. God understands mankind's inclination well.

The God Buzz

The phrase "God Buzz" may sound a little silly or strange to you, but this concept should be a core strategy for anything that requires momentum beyond what we are capable of creating with our own resources. For example, when I finish recording albums and start the marketing process for them, the God Buzz is a major element. What is the God Buzz? It is the momentum and "favorable wind" that God puts behind our efforts. After we've used every last drop of our available resources to push and promote something or achieve some feat, rest assured that God will come alongside us and create awareness for what we have done, if we keep him first. An entrepreneur can work hard and do everything in their power to bring an excellent product to market. God then takes that product to places they didn't even imagine it could reach. So we should always pray for and expect the "God Buzz" to kick in and move our activities even further.

Working With God in Tandem

Accuracy in life is connected to partnering with God. This means that man is to regularly submit his God-given plans to God and allow Him to make adjustments whenever and however He chooses. Ultimately, it is not man's plan that succeeds anyway, but God's (check out Proverbs 19:21). So it is wise to work with Him and let Him lead you toward your vision. We don't see the terrain as well as God does, nor do we even understand our own vision as well as God does. Therefore, it pays to have a partner who has the foresight to steer the ship in the right direction.

Now that we see the main reasons why our visions can overwhelm us, we can move past focusing on our obstacles and begin to move toward our goals. To realize our vision; we must undergo a process of personal growth because we can't bring about what we envision through our current resources, we must bring community into our vision (because we can't accomplish our vision alone), and we must rely on God's help (a God-given vision takes God's assistance), then we are ready to proceed with putting our vision into action.

Make the Vision Clear

Nothing will drive you (and those around you) more crazy than having a vision that is obscure. If you are like me, you think big and sometimes it's hard to quantify or make the vision that we have specific. If we can't make what we see very specific then we don't have a vision, we have a glimpse. A vision is something that you can put a plan behind and accomplish. A glimpse is a piece of the puzzle, something that leads to your larger vision. It is important to know the difference. Sometimes a vision is so big that there will be parts of it that we can make clear and other areas that you will have to revisit. The project management world calls this "rolling wave planning." Only certain aspects of the project can be planned because of limited information. Planning that requires additional knowledge is postponed. It is one thing to see that you will someday have great influence in your city (glimpse). It is

> *Vision is something that we evolve into. If we stay on God's path for our lives we will be taken through many life lessons that equip us to fulfill our vision in increasing measure.*

altogether a different and more powerful thing to see that you will become the mayor of your city by age 35 (vision). Living based off a glimpse can take us several different directions until it makes our heads spin. A clear vision gives us a plan of action and determines what choices need to be made in order to accomplish what we see.

If you only have a glimpse right now, don't put undue pressure on yourself to create a vision out of thin air. As I stated earlier, vision should be God-given and it will eventually come. God ultimately decides when He will unveil His vision for you. The most important part of the equation is to be open to letting God give us a vision. I have personally discovered that my vision is comprised of several different glimpses that have come to me throughout my life. I was able to recognize the patterns and sort of piece them together (I'm still getting glimpses, by the way). Several of these glimpses have been confirmed in my heart to such a degree that I have intelligent confidence to launch out on certain aspects of my vision. There are still certain portions of my vision that I wouldn't dare strike out on yet, realizing that certain things have to develop a little more before I try to make them reality. These are soft spots in my vision that are not clear yet (still in glimpse form).

Vision is something that we evolve into. If we stay on God's path for our lives we will be taken through many life lessons that equip us to fulfill our vision in increasing measure. You will begin to articulate your vision clearly to others and that is about 80 percent of the battle. Once we clearly verbalize what our vision consists of, it will be much easier to garner the resources and confidence needed to accomplish it. It is a beautiful thing when we begin to see people of different backgrounds and skill sets gather around a vision. There are all sorts of people who there who are hungry for a worthwhile vision to get behind and help push forward. There have been times when I had to tell people with whom I shared my sight to slow down because they were more ready than I was to undertake it at the time.

When Support for Your Vision Is Minimal

Don't be surprised if your vision attracts little support initially, especially if it's your first venture. Dr. John C. Maxwell in his classic work, *The 21 Irrefutable Laws of Leadership*, discusses the "Law of Buy-In," which states that "people have to buy into the leader first and the vision second." This concept gives voice to what many visionaries struggle with: lack of support. Even seasoned visionaries get hit by the rocky waves of diminished support from others in some seasons, especially if the course they are charting goes against the status quo.

If you know that your vision is a Godsend, you cannot always wait for people to get behind you before you pursue it. There are times when we must step out and risk looking foolish to those around us. By diligently working on what has been placed in our hearts to build, we will slowly gain momentum. There have been projects of mine (recent ones) that didn't get virtually any non-family member support until it was completed. I had to give the people something tangible to rally around before they offered their resources. This reality hurts sometimes, but it is something you will have to face and overcome if you want to see your vision come to pass. It's called building a track record. It is similar to a potential employer wanting to see your résumé, which clues them in on what you bring to the table and the results you've delivered.

The good news is that once you get into the habit of going after your vision without the initial support of others, you develop an inner resilience that becomes inspiring and magnetic. One day you'll look up and ask yourself, "Where in the world did all these new people come from?" I've gotten some of my greatest support mid-way through to the final stretch (when support is needed most) of various projects that I was working on. Many people are risk averse and they want to make sure that their investment of time and resources is put to good use. People who have something of value to give aren't quick to attach their reputations to things outside of themselves these days; you have to earn their trust first.

Early in my music career, I remember getting so frustrated about people not supporting and responding to my work the way I wanted them to. Later on in my journey, a very astute acquaintance of mine simply stated that I had to give people a reason to care about what I was doing. Those words of wisdom have stuck with me for years, especially when I find myself discouraged when my reward doesn't seem to match my labor. We can't pound our fists in anger if people don't get behind us (like I have been guilty of in the past). Though it can be heartbreaking and very disappointing when we don't see people championing our efforts, we must overcome the temptation to become bitter. Do not let your emotions get the best of you in this phase of your progress; it will only do more harm than good. Instead, take a walk and find a trustworthy person you can vent to about your frustrations. Get a clear head and perspective on where you are in your vision's process and keep trucking!

You always have to remember that a vision is something that you carry inside of you. Even when you articulate it and show tangible results from it, the vision resides in you. So that means that it will take others some time to warm up to our ideas, concepts and results. If it's a new undertaking and people don't know me from Joe Blow, it will take a little more time to get the strength of the people. That's just the way the world works. One thing to remember though is God can always intervene and cause us to have support that doesn't even make sense. But you will find that many times He allows us to go through processes naturally while He guides us.

You've Accomplished Your Vision ... Now What?

So you've accomplished an aspect of your ever-expanding vision — now what? I've made the mistake in the past of just rushing off to work on the next thing after I've completed another. It's partially my personality type and partially ignorance. It is important that once we finish an aspect of our vision, we do something to celebrate that victory. It is also important that we allow ourselves time to rest and reflect. You want to celebrate after every vision's victory because it brings closure to your mind, body and soul for that particular aspect of the journey. We have to condition our own minds. We may know from an intellectual level that we have completed something, but our minds, bodies and souls have been conditioned to keep going at the pace they were running while we were diligently working on the vision. You need something tangible to tell you that aspect of the race is finished and it's time to move on to another track. Think of it as the cool-down period on the treadmill after an intense cardio workout.

> *Rest allows our minds, bodies and souls to cool down and stop laboring. Periods of rest allow us to replenish emotional and mental energy.*

Celebration sends positive chemicals throughout the brain that will associate the completion of a task with good feelings. These good feelings are imperative because it provides us with fuel for the next part of our journey. Always keep track of your milestones; you will need them when you find yourself at places of discouragement when working on your next vision. Another important aspect of celebration is that it allows others to commemorate your victory, which is key in garnering future support. Let's face it: People love victories and winners. An event of some sort highlighting your accomplishment positions you as a winner in their minds and they will be more apt to get behind you on the next go round. You have proven that you have the juice to complete something that you said you would do (not an easy thing these days). A celebration also allows for us to see how many people actually did support us throughout our process that we did not recognize. It's hard to tell who is for you and who is against you when you are in the trenches. But also beware that people who don't support you will show up to your party as well (but still be gracious and welcome them to sip some victory champagne, too).

Secondly, we want to allow ourselves a period of rest after we bring a major vision to fruition. Rest in this sense is not necessarily sleep (though that is part of it). Rest allows our minds, bodies and souls to cool down and stop laboring. Periods of rest allow us to replenish emotional and mental energy. I find that I'm at my best sometimes when I forego extensive preparation in favor of just relaxing and taking it easy. I love Stephen R. Covey's concept of "sharpening the saw" found in his classic book, *The 7 Habits of Highly Effective People*. He speaks of the importance of self-renewal in the areas of physical, mental, social/emotional and spiritual health. Covey opens the chapter with a story about a man, who is trying to cut down a tree with an ax, but the man is tired and the ax is becoming dull. When another man suggests that he take a break and sharpen his saw, the tree cutter refuses, saying he doesn't have time. Covey points out that the tree cutter dulls his effectiveness by continuing to hack away at the tree without resting.

Sadly, this is the attitude of our modern culture, especially with the more ambitious types. We don't take the time to take care of our greatest asset: ourselves. Thus, we find ourselves worn down, exhausted and beat up even while experiencing great victories. God himself rested from all of His labor. If the Creator felt it was important to take a load off, how much more should we, his fallible creation? Rest is a time for you to find your center again. The pursuit of vision and the quest of living an accurate life can be draining. Furthermore, it is impossible to live an accurate life without learning the art of relaxing. We all need time to recuperate so that we can remain on target. Rest brings us back to a place of remembering why we do what we are doing in the first place. We will end up exhausted if we go from project to project, accomplishment to accomplishment, or victory to victory, without a break in between.

World-class athletes are sometimes terrified of gruesome game schedules that provide only small periods of rest. They know that in order to be at their best, they have to allow their bodies time to recalibrate. I remember watching a Kobe Bryant interview one year after the Los Angeles Lakers had won the Western Conference Championship. The Eastern Conference Finals were still undecided. The reporter asked Bryant what he was going to do with all the time they had off before the NBA Championship. He replied, "rest," with a smile and an exhausted sigh of relief. It was as if some huge boulder had been taken off of his shoulders and before going back into battle.

I love the concept of the Sabbath. Reggie McNeal provides a thorough understanding of the Sabbath in his book, *Practicing Greatness*. He states, "God instituted Sabbath to give people rest, which involves more dimensions that just physical relief. In biblical terms the day is designed to disrupt life's usual routines to allow people the opportunity to remember and reflect. We do well to remember that our lives are being lived against the backdrop of eternity, that we are created by God to enjoy him. Given this remembrance we can then reflect on the status of our lives." You may or may not be a person of faith, but a period of rest (or Sabbath) is one of the unseen laws that govern humankind. Many people try to disregard this law and do so at the expense of their health, relationships and overall well-being.

There is a very foolish concept floating around many ambitious circles known as "no days off." This idea is meant to convey that if you rest you will not advance to where you want to be in life. The "no days off" mindset may sound motivating and inspiring, but it will be a major component in the demise of those who practice it. Realistically, it's impossible to not take a breather. Either you'll be wise enough to incorporate rest into your life or your body and/or some other unforeseen circumstance will force you to take a vacation.

McNeal accurately explains that rest allows us the opportunity to reflect on the condition of our lives. Reflection is imperative for accuracy. We all must take self-inventory to see our progress or lack thereof. The day-to-day grind of life can be a dog fight, especially if you are trying to live accurately. While in that battle, it is hard to recognize what's going wrong and what is going right. Reflection is a pause in the filming of your life's movie that allows you to judge if the scenes are going according to the script. If we don't reflect, we may find ourselves filming the wrong movie. We are able to re-check our motives when we take a brief escape from day-to-day activities. All people lose their way at times; therefore, we all need reminders of the core values that caused us to pursue the things that we're striving to attain.

Jesus Christ is famous for having gone to lonely places to pray, meditate and be renewed. He had a gigantic vision He was sent to accomplish and one of the reasons He was able to finish His assigned work was because He took the time to reflect, especially after He experienced major victories. Reflection and rest are core strategies that will enable us to stay on track as we position ourselves for the next phase of the vision.

Vision is truly a gift from God because it gives mankind a sense of meaning. It is a great feeling to envision something and then be able to feast our eyes and ears on it once it becomes reality. As you pursue your vision, keep in mind that it is a privilege to do so and don't give up until you accomplish it. Keep your vision in front of you regularly and share it with trustworthy people who will hold you accountable and encourage you along the way. Consult with God about the vision that He has placed inside of you. Communicate with Him on a daily basis through prayer to determine whether or not you are building according to the right plans. He will provide you with the favorable winds and all of the resources necessary to bring what is in your mind and heart out to the people who will benefit most from it. Your vision should always be something that improves the well-being of others. Speak positively about your vision to yourself. Even when it looks like things are at their worst, continue to tell yourself that you will accomplish it. The power of life (positive creation) and of death (decay and destruction) resides in your tongue (in what you communicate both externally and internally). The majority of the battle related to realizing vision is fought in your mind. If you think negative thoughts (death), it will be impossible to produce (give life to) what's inside of you.

Application of Accuracy

- Keep your vision in sight and continually remind yourself of it.
- Consult with God frequently about your mission to make sure you are on track.
- Ask trustworthy people to hold you accountable for your vision.
- Speak positively about your vision.

CHAPTER 3

Knowing Who You Are

How does knowing who we are relate to living an accurate life? Knowledge of our identity is paramount to traveling the path of accuracy. I'm about to make some layered statements in this chapter, so please bear with me as we dive a little deeper into this. Lack of identity will lead to an aimless, unfulfilled and confused life. One of the most profound assaults on my generation lies in trying to keep us from knowing who we were created to be.

People who suffer with identity issues are much easier to manipulate and be swayed from their proper lane in life. Show me someone who is insecure and bends whichever way life tells them to (or are utterly stubborn) and more than likely I will show you someone who does not know who they are. Many of us find ourselves in places, relationships and situations where we put on masks in order to fit in. We wear these disguises for so long that we can lose ourselves in the process. We end up doing things and going down paths never intended for us because we feel as though we have to be something we're not. The reason for this (at times) is not necessarily that people feel they aren't good enough, but that they don't know who they are in the first place.

You will always succumb to the pressure to conform into who you are not if you don't get a good grasp of who your Creator wired you to be. We will always operate off of whatever information we have. If the information we have about ourselves is inaccurate — guess what — the majority of our actions will be too. Individuals are not the only ones who suffer from problems that stem from false identity. Families, cities, states, nations, churches, businesses and people groups suffer when they don't have a sense of who they are collectively.

What Database Do You Live From?

People have a lot in common with computers or, rather, computers have a lot in common with us. The programming (information) instilled in a person will always determine what they will act on in the long run. As stated earlier, I am not a doom and gloom kind of guy, but the majority of the information fed to us on a daily basis is inaccurate and/or used to rope us into mental paradigms that enslave us. Now, this is a bold statement and almost sounds like conspiracy thought. However you take it, it is true. There is a real system at work that seeks to make as many people slaves and ultimately self-destruct. The way it is marketed makes it appear innocent and actually good for us, but behind the cover-up hides very wicked intent.

I am a very open-minded person and I have a healthy interest in different types of music, literature, art, points of view and other mediums. Yet, I am very cautious with how I take in different forms of information because it can skew the programming that guides my life. To take this thought even further, even "good" information can become harmful if we do not control how we receive it. If we want to live an accurate life, we must first seek out God and let Him guide us through the process of personal discovery. God formed every part of us; that includes mind, body, soul and spirit. He knows the desires in our hearts, the talents he gave us and what we are capable of doing.

There is a system in this world diametrically opposed to God's plan for your life that seeks to slowly entice you away from His perfect destination. This world system perpetuates inaccurate information to derail destinies. Many of us find ourselves living according to the wrong information that this system pushes on us because it is loud and it is everywhere. Proverbs 9:13 states, "The woman Folly is loud, she is undisciplined and without knowledge." In this passage, folly, or foolishness, represents the corrupt informational system that opposes God. There are only three databases that we have to choose from, either God's wisdom, corrupt world system, or our own very limited and highly inaccurate personal experience.

I regularly see the lives that are negatively affected by the influence of folly and the choice to follow its path. Many identities are getting shaped by inaccurate sources of information and even though some who buy into this farce may look successful, their lives are just smoke and mirrors. The folly database is much easier to follow than the wisdom of God because we live in a world where foolishness is embraced and advertised on a regular basis. You can't turn on the television without getting a glimpse of it. Remember, if a lie is touted as the truth for long enough, it will eventually be accepted as truth if a person doesn't develop a close intimacy with authentic truth. Now I'm not advocating a boycott on television, the Internet and other forms of media. Yet, I am a strong proponent of being grounded in truth in order to better recognize the real from the fake.

Who Are You?

The "Who are you?" question is one that you will be presented with frequently. As I stated earlier, the single largest battle in the war of living an accurate life is that of identity. The decisions we make daily, even the small ones, have their roots tied directly to who we think we are. There are things that some people will absolutely refuse to do because it doesn't line up with their internal perception. In order to have high standards for our lives, we must know who we are. In order to know who we are, we must know who God is.

God is the author of life. The wisdom he provides is what guides people of influence to make correct decisions. Proverbs 8:15-16 powerfully points out that, "by me kings reign and rulers issue decrees that are just; by me princes govern, and nobles — all who rule on earth." All of this is a fancy way of saying that wherever you find someone making accurate choices and executing properly targeted plans, you will find the wisdom of God. This is the type of information you won't see in commercials and advertisements. It pays to learn who God is through an ever-maturing relationship with Him. We are created in God's image and it takes a lifetime to be molded into His likeness.

There was a point in my life where I really did not know who I was. I'm still learning who I am in many respects, but now I have a much better handle on what my identity is. During this period of identity crisis, I came to the realization that I had tried to find my identity in everyone and everything except God. I was brought to a place of despair and utter emptiness. People with this issue find themselves doing all sorts of things to fill the void in their souls.

The more I discovered who God is, the more He revealed to me who I was. After I digested this information, I was left with the choice to either keep or discard my sense of false identity. This was a very long process, and to this day there are still remnants of my old false identity that I have to face and abandon (the parts of me that are not like Him). At the end of the day, I would not trade my true and accurate identity for the old misled one.

So who are you? Though you may not be able to articulate the answer easily, there should be something in your inner core that evokes peace if and when that question is posed. If not, that is a sign that a stronger connection with the Heavenly Father needs to be built. Furthermore, you won't have to strive to come up with an identity when you are in close proximity with God regularly. You will feel less pressure to prove yourself, a feeling that stems from insecurity, which stems from lack of confidence in who we are.

Be Who You Are Meant to Be

> *In order to have high standards for our lives, we must know who we are. In order to know we are, we must know who God is.*

There will always be a tremendous amount of pressure to conform into who others want you to be. And while we should be flexible and make adjustments if it makes us a better person, we must fight to discover, develop and maintain our core identity. I have a lot of friends who are angry with themselves for listening to other people instead of following their hearts regarding what path they should have chosen for their lives. It's a terrible feeling to know that you have not fulfilled being the best you that you can be and traded that possibility in to please someone else. We all have a niche to fill in this life. Everything from your personality, background and experiences, to your talents, mentality and passions were ingredients God put in you to do something special in the earth.

If you try to be someone else, then you will end up doing the world a terrible disservice. I should add that it is important to work on our character flaws and negative quirks. The parts of us that benefit the world are the good parts of us. Though you want to be authentically you, don't get a "this is just the way I am" type of attitude. We want to become the greatest version of ourselves that we are meant to be.

A lot of who we are has to do with our gifts, talents and passions. People are prone to give their life to what they are passionate about. The skills we develop and the talents we naturally possess are great indicators that show where our greatest places of impact may be. In the first chapter of this book, I discussed impact and how that is a major component of living an accurate life. Being who you are meant to be will set you up for your platform to make the greatest impact that you can.

The Wrong Armor

Back to David for a moment. I love the story about David and Goliath and I believe it illustrates the importance of being true to who God made us to be. David was a wise young man before he was ever promoted to the king of Israel because he understood the importance and value in being himself. Let me paint a picture for you to illustrate a point. At the time, Goliath, the great champion and 9-foot-tall behemoth of a man, had the entire army of Israel shaking in its boots as he challenged them to produce a warrior that could face him in one-on-one combat. No one in all of Israel was up for the challenge except the teenager David, who wasn't even in the army. He was a shepherd boy who was running an errand for his father who asked him to check on his three brothers who were in Israel's army. Long story short, David caught wind of the giant's insults and saw that none of his fellow Israelites were willing to take on Goliath. So David accepted the challenge. Saul, who was king of Israel at that time, was excited that this naïve youngster would take the heat and face the behemoth.

King Saul urged David to wear his own personal armor. David put it on, but it was too heavy for him and he knew he wouldn't be able to fight in it. He decided to face Goliath in his regular clothes, armed only with a sling shot and five smooth stones. When he approached Goliath, the giant laughed at him and continued his barrage of insults. David was not intimidated, though, and skillfully hit the champion of the Philistines smack-dab in the middle of the forehead. This knocked Goliath off of his feet, and David then took the giant's own sword and cut his head off with it. I'm sure jaws dropped on both sides of the battle field. Pardon the old mafia lingo but this snot-nosed shepherd boy whacked one of the greatest warriors on the planet at that time. It was a great feat.

David was true to himself and who God made him to be. He didn't try to fight Goliath as a soldier of Israel or as some great warlord. He came as a shepherd boy who was passionate about the honor of his God and his people, who was skillful with a sling shot. David had a lot of help from God, might I add. Young David had a clear concept of who he was, even at a young age. He was able to lean on this information when it counted the most. If the lad had gone out in King Saul's armor, tailored specifically for him, David would have been killed. He had great confidence in God and who God revealed him to be. That's why he didn't cave into the pressure to be someone other than himself.

I think he realized that he had a better shot at defeating the giant by executing what he had spent several years already cultivating. The story of David and Goliath is a favorite among many people, especially those who consider themselves underdogs. I'd even venture to say that those who seek to live an accurate life are this world's underdogs. Almost everything and everyone is betting against us. The path of accuracy requires courage because it means going against what the majority erroneously accepts as correct. I'm sure as David stepped out on the battlefield to square off with Goliath, even his own kinsman probably thought he was crazy and started thinking about what they were going to say at David's funeral. But David chose the path of accuracy when it counted the most; with the help of his God, he resolved to be himself despite both internal and external tension to do otherwise.

You have to be whom you were meant to be, especially in times of crisis. Many people lose their way when they are faced with a drastic change because they begin to rely on the armor of King Saul rather than the tested and approved sling and stones they used when no one was watching them. Resolve to be who you are meant to be while in private and you will experience great victories publicly.

In What Areas Are You Gifted?

Knowing what we are gifted at plays an important role in knowing who you are. Our identities and the paths that we take in life are inextricably linked to whatever gifts we've been given. A gift is God-given and is something that you naturally do well. It is fairly easy to identify what your gifts are because people will usually point them out to you. If you hear enough compliments about something you do naturally, without exerting much effort, that is a strong indication of giftedness.

Some gifts may take longer than others to discover, but everyone has a gift nonetheless. Perhaps you have an uncanny way of connecting with people, or you're really good at solving problems, or maybe you're really good at putting together outfits. These are examples of gifts and are part of what makes you, well, you. You will find that you are most fulfilled when you are using your gifts as oppose to using a set of skills that you picked up along the way.

Once you have discovered your gift, you should exercise it regularly so that it can be developed, recognized and offered to God so that He can take you as far as he would like with it. There is no purpose in having a gift if it remains unused and unshared with others for their benefit. Gifts and character should be developed simultaneously. There are a lot of tremendously gifted people out there who lack sufficient character to keep them where their gifting places them. It takes a very wise, self-aware and humble individual to allow God to build up their character before they go after the opportunities that giftedness present.

Since our gifts are a very integral part of who we are, it should be worked deeply into the fabric of our awareness. There are countless people who just sit on their gifts and are miserable as a result. If we don't exercise our gifts on a regular basis, we will lose part of who we are. Alternatively, we grow increasingly confident in who we are the more we use our gifts.

What Are Your Talents?

Talents are very similar to gifts, but there's a difference. A gift is usually a passionate ability that comes naturally. A talent, on the other hand, can be something that you are good at (or have great potential to be good at) but you could take it or leave it in terms of whether it is used or not. For example, someone may be a gifted singer and she feel as though she cannot breathe if she's not singing. This same person is a very talented songwriter, but doing so is a challenge; however, she can sing like a bird without much effort. Talents are just as important as gifts because they are complementary partners. Honing a talent makes us just that much better at executing our gifts. Many people make the mistake of just focusing on their gifts and not spending time developing their accompanying talents. Not only will they have to give an account to their Creator for this waste of resources He placed in them, their identity will also suffer as a result.

Talents are part of who we are too. God wouldn't have given them to us if they weren't important. I believe there are certain seasons of life where our gifts aren't the prominent expressions we will be able to use, but our talents are. For example, pretend that the singer that I mentioned earlier ended up having to get throat surgery and was unable to sing for several months. She still would be able to write songs if she had been exercising this important talent. It would drive this same singer crazy had she not given herself another outlet of self-expression. Knowing your talents will give you an even greater focus as it pertains to your direction in life. Having a love for singing and the ability to do so is great. Yet, combining that information and ability with the talent to network, build business models and do graphic design, for instance, will propel her into even greater success. A gift alone can take you down several paths that may or may not be accurate for your life, but you are more likely to find your niche if you couple your gifts with well-developed talents.

What Are You Passionate About?

Our gifts and talents can be viewed as the self-identifying tools that we possess. Our passion is the area of life where we desire to use these tools. What are you willing to give your life to? What makes you angry? What motivates you? The overlapping answer to these three questions is a good indicator of where your passion is (and the path you should follow). Passion is less about what you do and more about who you are.

The gifts and talents we possess shine brightest when we apply them toward people and causes we are passionate about. Sure, we may lend our gifts and talents to other things from time to time; however, they ultimately belong to the desire of our hearts. True passion is never extinguished. Though it may become discouraged and even be suppressed every now and then, it remains a part of who we are because God placed it there.

Every day that I wake up I am driven to realize my full God-given potential and teach others how to do the same. That concept is not just something I'm passionate about; it is part of my internal make-up. I couldn't change this facet of myself if I wanted to. No matter what interests I've had throughout the years, realizing my full God-given potential lies at the heart of pretty much everything I do. Anything that doesn't add to that passion eventually dries up for me. An understanding of what you are passionate about will make clearer what opportunities to take or leave.

True passion is a consistent theme in our lives. No matter what happens in life, good or bad, a person will still desire their passion if it is authentic. That is what we want to find, true passion, because there lays one of the hallmark elements of our identity. Show me a person who knows what her passion is and I will show you someone who is well acquainted with who they are (or on the right path to discover who they are). I should add that God is the one who shows us the ultimate passions of our heart. Money, fame, and power are limited pursuits because human beings is wired to be fulfilled by something much greater, God Himself.

At the root of all true passion is eternity. There are some passions in our heart that you and I aren't even able to clearly describe to others. Some of the frustrations people have are from them sensing a void or having a desire to produce something that doesn't exist yet. Steve Jobs, the late co-founder and CEO of Apple Inc., had a burning desire to create a computer that would be like an extension of the human body. Beyond that, he wanted to create a culture of continuous innovation. Under Jobs' leadership, Apple became more than a run-of-the-mill computer manufacturer — it became a lifestyle brand. The Apple empire embodies his passion. For Jobs, Apple was not only a company, but a vehicle to leave a dent in the universe.

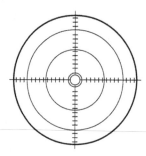

Scope of Accuracy – Steve Jobs

Steve Jobs was more than a tech magnate, he was a revolutionary. His passion and drive for greatness led to groundbreaking products such as the iPad which sold over a quarter of a billion units, the iMac Computer which sold over 6 million units, and the Pixar/Disney movie franchise "Toy Story" which sold 350 million worldwide during its initial release. Steve Jobs was a model of resiliency and determination. He was ousted by the board of directors and 10 years later was brought back as CEO when he sold his new company, NeXT, to Apple for more than $400 million.

Jobs had a unique way of balancing huge ambition with pragmatism and this is what led to his survival during the years he struggled with his new company Next. Steve Jobs was willing to risk his personal finances in order to ensure the success of his startup ventures, one of which was Pixar. Jobs was also not one to wing it or leave success up to chance. He practiced and practiced before he did his Apple World presentations and was notorious for drilling his employees if they had any part to play in them. Jobs aimed for perfection and accepted nothing less than amazing results from his team.

You must find the deep burning passion placed within you if you are to gain a greater understanding of who you are. People with a mature passion walk a very narrow course that leads them to their true destiny. Mature passion has been tested and tried by the storms, distractions and fog of life. People who don't have something that they are willing to give their life to are aimless. Furthermore, lack of knowledge of one's passion will likely result in having less of an impact.

Personality

It is wise to know your personality, or how you are wired. The best two ways to get this information is asking those who know you the best and personality tests. Your temperament, natural inclinations and outlook on life are all parts of your personality. Some of the better personality tests that I have found are the Myers-Brigg and Jung. These particular tests also have free versions available online that are pretty accurate and informative. There are an abundance of personality tests that you can take online by doing a simple Google search.

There are quirks that each one of us has that provide insight into which of life's lanes that best suits us. This is not to say that we may end up somewhere and doing something totally different than what we expect.

What Are Your Strengths?

Uncovering our strengths is critical to knowing who we are. You don't want to find yourself doing something that is outside of your strength zone often. Strengths are your better personality traits. These are the qualities that we possess that have great value and help meet the needs of others who lack them. A great resource that can be used to help identify your strengths is the book *StrengthsFinder 2.0* by Tom Rath. I have found it to be very valuable when assessing what places and positions that best match my greatest assets. Another great resource is the book *Leading From Your Strengths* by John Trent, Rodney Cox and Eric Tooker.

Whenever we can help it, we always want to put ourselves in a position where our strengths can be utilized. Some of the most frustrating and disillusioned seasons of my life were the periods when I was not operating in my strengths. Granted, we can't always choose the course life takes us on; however, when it comes down to your own personal decision, select opportunities that will put your best parts to use.

Strengths, much like gifts and talents, must be further developed by exercising them regularly. You do others and yourself no service by just sitting on your superior qualities. Strengths should be used to enhance the quality of the relationships that you have. We should also seek to know the strengths of others so that we learn to depend on them in those areas (especially if we are deficient in those places). Humility and strength should always go hand in hand because we are all interdependent.

I am learning the habit of not comparing my strengths with those of others. It is counterproductive to do so. It is much more effective and worthwhile to know my deficiencies and seek to find those who possess strength where I'm weak. Strengths become weaknesses when we don't have a sober view of how to use them in connection to other people. Sadly, I have learned this the hard way many times. I am just now coming to grips with the concept of effective collaboration and welcoming the strength of others in the places that I am weak.

What Are Your Flaws and Weaknesses?

I usually find that people are on two opposite sides of the spectrum when it comes to knowing their flaws and weaknesses. Either they won't admit where they're deficient or they are obsessed with the bad parts of themselves. Neither of these sides are healthy. Knowing our flaws and weaknesses allows us to know where we need to improve and where we are to depend on others.

Flaws are the ugly qualities that we possess. They generally come from bad experiences in our lives that have left emotional scars. We all have flaws — there is only one perfect person that has ever lived and that is the Son of God, Jesus Christ. Therefore, we all have to get over our tendency to push the fact that we have flaws under the rug, refusing to admit that we have them. The next step is to begin to work on improving our blemished parts. We will only go as far as our weaknesses let us. Even if your strengths, talents and gifts take you to the moon, unchecked flaws will shoot you back down to Earth quicker than you can scratch you head.

Being flawed is just part of being human. Hence, they are something that we must seriously take into account when assessing who we are. It is healthy to get to a place where we are well aware of our flaws and are taking the actions necessary not to let them limit our fullest potential. It is not fun to look in the mirror and begin the work of self-discovery that uncovers our defects, but it can sometimes mean the difference between true success and irreparable failure. There are several gifted individuals who at one time commanded the world as their audience, but unmanaged flaws wrecked their influence. So get well acquainted with your ugly side and do the work necessary to make it a little easier on the emotional eyes. Flaws are inherent, but weaknesses remind us that we can't do anything of true significance without others.

Therefore, weaknesses can be viewed in a positive light. Though no one desires to be deficient, a weakness allows us to rely on people who are strong in those areas. A weakness is different than a flaw. A weakness may be due to not having a particular ability. That's great. No one can do everything. Rather, we should all strive to be great in whatever ability we have been blessed with. There are some weaknesses that have to be strengthened, regardless of whether we enjoy them or are even wired that way. For example, you may not be a people person but because we live in a world full of people, you are best served if you learn how to interact with others in a respectful manner. But there are other weaknesses where we should just say, "It is what it is," and find someone who can complement us in that area. People end up wasting valuable time trying to improve every weakness they have instead of developing their strengths.

The point is to know our weaknesses and to try to surround ourselves with others who can supplement those deficiencies. We must differentiate between the weaknesses that need to be strengthened and the ones that are OK to let be. We are able to gauge that by what is required of us in the sphere of influence in which we function. A truly strong person knows just as much about their weaknesses as they do

> *Strengths become weaknesses when we don't have a sober view of how to use them in connection to other people.*

their strengths. So it is important to have a firm grasp on both. To live an accurate life, you have to get good at being you, and part of that is recognizing both the good and bad parts of yourself.

Getting Comfortable in Your Own Skin

At the end of the day, the best gift you can give to the world is to just be yourself because you are awesome in your own way. Get comfortable in your own skin and be you. It is disheartening to see that so many of the people who I come across place a low value on themselves. No matter what they do or how many lives they touch, they feel as though they are not good enough. I find that many of these individuals are people pleasers and always end up being hurt in the long run, because you just can't please everyone. Even when you are at your best, some Joe Schmoe somewhere is going to point out why they think you're not great.

There comes a point where you have to realize that you are who you are and it is a great addition to the world. There will never be another soul exactly like you on this earth and there is a reason why you exist. Some people can't shake the negative things that have happened in their past and because of that they despise themselves. What happened in the past doesn't necessarily have to define your future. Even if there are consequences that come from your past, you can make the most of your today and still come out on top.

I heard a great communicator once say that it is easier to forgive others than it is to forgive ourselves. Don't let the mistakes you made yesterday or even today dictate the rest of your life. There is treasure inside of you that needs to be revealed to the people you're connected with. Your outlook, experiences, talents, gifts, strengths, flaws and weaknesses are all by divine design. There are people who will connect with your unique set of attributes.

Many of us exert our precious time and energy concentrating on what makes or made others great and we become unhappy with ourselves. In this sea of discontentment, we fail to realize the greatness lying under our own skin. Everyone needs a healthy dose of appreciation for themselves because we are fearfully and wonderfully made by a gracious God. Once I got the great epiphany that it was OK to be me, it revolutionized my life and made things a lot less complicated.

I stopped putting on a mask and started being transparent about who I was, with others and myself. Then I began to find that others felt like it was OK to truly be themselves around me because of that. In addition, authentic relationships were able to be formed because some people no longer felt the need to mask who they were. It was now real people forming a bond at the heart level. I'm sure you can imagine what a breath a fresh air this was for me and those I encountered during that time.

It takes courage to cross the threshold of becoming comfortable in your own skin. There is a whole world of people screaming at you to do otherwise. The crazy thing about that is that those same people screaming at you to do otherwise yearn to be accepted for who they truly are; they just lack the courage to trail blaze that path. Once you conquer your fear and begin to operate in your true design, the right people will find you because of the newfound freedom you walk in. Therefore, you are not the only one affected by your bravery and commitment to being comfortable with you. A person who is at home with themselves also realizes that they have flaws to work on and even weaknesses that must sometimes be strengthened (or supplemented). They embrace this, and then work hard to shine through their gifts, talents and strengths. He or she is also well aware of how they are wired and what that means for their environment.

Being comfortable with who you are does not mean taking on an air of arrogance as so many erroneously believe. On the contrary, it is a healthy understanding and confidence in who one is, acknowledging both positive and negative qualities. Those still trapped by fear will always point the finger at those who have conquered theirs. So once you get over your own cowardice and embrace who you are, you will continually have to make sure that you stay in that place. Yet, as stated earlier, there will be people who come out of the woodwork that are attracted to your revolutionary boldness.

Be a Better You

I have done my best to convey in this chapter that it is critical to know who you are in order to live an accurate life. Yet, one cannot stop here. Once you learn who you are, the next and never-ending step is to become a better you. Self-improvement is not only limited to enhancing your gifts, talents and strengths. Becoming a better person includes developing character, emotional health and understanding.

Character is not only who we are when people are looking, but who we are when no one else is around. Character is found in the small decisions we make on a daily basis. It is the power to choose right over wrong, or what is best over what is merely good. There is a power that resides in people of character, and it is magnified when they are in a crisis. The real you will always show up when you're in a crisis or other significant life transition. We always want to posture ourselves to be a people of noble character even during times of hardship and great success. It first starts with a heartfelt desire to be a person of great quality, then filling our hearts and minds with the right information on the regular, making decisions based on that information (with God's guidance as the center piece), and surrounding ourselves with people who have a track record of excellent character. It benefits us just as much as other people when we have solid character. You become a joy to be around because of your reliable, trustworthy and honest nature. There is also less fear in a person who knows they are truthful.

Emotional Health

Emotional health is often an overlooked virtue in North American culture. We spend so much of our time on the American dream and the pursuit of happiness, that we often forego any thought to our emotional wellbeing as we chase after these things. Even communities of faith sacrifice emotional health to gain what they consider success. As you pursue an accurate life, emotional health is a critical part of the equation. There are a lot of people who achieved accuracy in certain areas of their lives, but they are emotional dwarves. A great book on this topic is *Emotionally Healthy Spirituality* by Peter Scazzero. This writing comingles two topics that are rarely joined together, but need to be more often. It is hard to truly have one without the other. Emotionally healthy people are mature and are able to own up to their mistakes. They are also able to properly handle conflict and process varying information from a stable perspective. I have found in my own experience that emotional health must be learned, practiced and cultivated. Emotional health, much like character is something that is intentionally developed over time. Those who are emotionally healthy are able to open themselves up to get a true understanding of others.

Understanding is the skill to make accurate decisions based on acquiring the right information. An example of understanding is a husband reading the body language of his wife that tells him she had a hard day at work, so based off that information he cooks dinner for the family instead of asking her. I'm sure you can imagine that living life this way is a breath of fresh air to those who are around you on a consistent basis. Gaining understanding, or wisdom, comes both from experience and the hand of God. There are some things I just know because God has revealed them, others I received knowledge of by bumping my head or succeeding on accident. Not everybody utilizes understanding though it is available to us all. It is impossible to employ understanding if we are full of our own opinions and knowledge. We gain understanding by being around those who have a greater measure of it than we do.

You Learn Who You Are by Being in God's Presence

Someone wise once told me that if you want to know who you are, go to the one who created you. This simple yet profound statement transformed my approach to discovering my true identity. Just think about it for a minute: If you want to know how something works, the best person to ask would be the engineer or manufacturer. I used things, experiences and people to define who I was and it always left a void. It wasn't until I began to get to know God that I truly began to get to understand my true self. Since He created me, it makes sense that He would know me the best.

Self-discovery is inextricably linked to God discovery. The more we learn who God is, the more we learn who we truly are. Many of the identities that people find themselves wearing are counterfeits. The truth is that we cannot be defined totally by what we do, the clothes we wear, where we live, our net worth, or our network of relationships. At the end of the day we all come from God. He is the source of our origin and the only being that has the capacity to reveal and give us our identity. There will always be a huge void in the hearts of people who don't look to God to find out who they are. Human beings are complex and we were created to be defined by much more than this earth can offer.

There is an authentic confidence that comes when we find ourselves in God. This confidence is unshakeable because it does not depend on our performance or image (which we use to impress people). God could care less about these things; He is much more interested in us. Therefore, the shallow things that the majority of people use to define who they are dissolve when they come into contact with a perfect being that sees beyond that. When I first came to encounter God in a real way, it scared me to death because I realized all of the crutches that I leaned on for my identity didn't make a difference to Him. My reputation and accomplishments were good things, but those didn't benefit God any. God peers into our hearts and souls and reveals the hidden parts within us that we don't even know about. True identity is found in the deep recesses within us, not the shallow pools that we use to gain human acceptance.

Out of the life of God flows everything. He is the essence of all things and nothing would exist without Him. So just imagine how amazing it would be to stay in the presence of the source of life every day. The life that we have been given was never meant to be lived apart from God. Similarly, our identities were never meant to be found in detachment from Him either. Mankind has a lot of pride though; many of us hate the thought of being defined by someone else. I struggle with this myself. Often, God has to show his creation how empty and confusing life is without Him. King Solomon, one of the wisest and wealthiest rulers to ever walk the face of the earth even acknowledged how vain life is without a true connection to God. He expressed in his book found in the Bible, Ecclesiastes, that life is a mere chasing after the wind without a deep-rooted foundation built upon God.

He goes on to discuss that he accomplished major feats, denied himself no pleasure under the sun and filled himself with all kinds of knowledge, but in the end it proved to be worthless without God. Solomon would be on the Forbes list year after if he were alive today. If a man who had that much wealth and wonderful life experiences can testify that a life without God is vain, we should heed his advice.

The world that we live in has been fooled into thinking that it can find its identity without God. It is the old carrot on a stick trick; it keeps pursuing something that it will never be able to obtain. If you and I are not careful, we will fall into the same mode of thinking without even knowing it because much of the information circulating around is centered on discovering who we are apart from God. I should also add that the hustle and bustle of life can crowd out the most important time of our day, the portion that should be spent with absolute focus on God. Busyness or the rat race, as some call it; will so entangle us that we lose our center. We have to fight to remain aware of our God-given identities and vigilantly keep guard against the identities this misled world system seeks to trap us in. There is always a counterfeit identity that we can put on, and it takes a daily concentrated effort to operate in the real one.

You Learn Who You Are Through Meaningful Relationships with Others

After we gain our true identity in God, there is the next step of fine tuning and refining who we are by interacting with other people on a regular basis. We can learn a lot about ourselves when we come into contact with other people. It's always fun to see what happens when I introduce myself to a new social circle. Well, maybe not always fun, but it is interesting. There are quirks, talents and other parts of us that are only realized when we get around others. God gives us the confidence in who we are and people give us the environment to express who we are.

Beware of just trying to be a loner while discovering who you are (at least not for a long period of time). We become weird and very emotionally unhealthy when we try to function solely by ourselves. Being around people offers balance and different perspectives that are sometimes better than our own. There have been several occasions where I thought my outlook on a particular situation was accurate, but once I spoke about it in public I got wise feedback that made me reevaluate my thinking.

God provides us with an awareness of our ultimate value, but he uses people to express that value to us in a way that makes it tangible for us. There are things that we just can't hope to know about ourselves if it is not tested in the fire of interaction with other people.

> *There is an authentic confidence that comes when we find ourselves in God. This confidence is unshakeable because it does not depend on our performance or image (which we use to impress people).*

I have found that there has to be a balance in letting God reveal our identities and what I let people confirm my identity as. God created us to be interdependent. So it makes sense that we find some of our value in our identification with outside people.

We never want to let other people define who we are (that is God's job), but other people can confirm and even encourage us in regard to the identity He has already given. I've become even more aware of who I am by forming deep bonds with friends in recent years. I also keep a good handle on what is part of my purpose by working with younger men that I have been called to help develop. There are certain parts of who I am that are discerned when I am with my family. All of these different relationships in my life form a beautiful collage that expresses my God given identity and will do the same for you.

If you are an introvert like me, you will have to take pains to step out of your comfort zone and try to establish healthy relational ties with new people not in your usual circle. That is one of the surest ways to grow as a person. Introverts typically have a strong concept of self and rely less on the opinions of others to affirm them. We sometimes can become disillusioned as a result and lose our proper grip on reality. Introverts typically form deep bonds with a few people that they get to know very well. This limits us because the greater number of quality people we can surround ourselves with, the more accurate our perspectives can become.

Extroverts, alternatively, may have to learn how not to rely so heavily on the approval of others. Since most extroverts naturally love to be around people, it makes sense that they derive a large dose of their identity from connecting with others. It can be hard to navigate life when your objective is to please people. There is a good chance that you will miss your opportunity to be accurate in order to ensure that the many lives you associate with are happy, which is impossible.

Keeping in mind the knowledge of being an introvert or extrovert will serve us well as we look to confirm our identities by relating to other people. Just remember that God is the ultimate source for your identity. I have to constantly remind myself of this fact. We've discussed knowing who you are in this chapter. Next we will dive deeper into relational dynamics and how those pertain to an accurate life.

Application of Accuracy

- **Continually examine and scrutinize the database that you live from, as it will determine your long term habits.**
- **Because we learn who we are by learning and experiencing who God is, make time to spend with God through prayer (conversation), reading His book (the Bible) and hanging out with others who really know Him.**
- **Be authentically you — quirks, strengths, weaknesses and all. You exist for a reason. Some things we must improve without losing who we are in the process.**
- **Discover your gifts and talents and put them to use.**
- **Find what you are passionate about and do it.**
- **Be a better you.**

SECTION II

RELATIONSHIPS

Through relationships we find our sense of belonging. One of the surest ways to damage a person (either physically or emotionally) is to completely isolate them from others. Therefore much of what pertains to life is found in the quality of our connections with other people. In this section, I seek to lay groundwork for accuracy as it pertains to our relationship with God, spouses, family, dating interests, friends, community, associates and our enemies.

CHAPTER 4

God, Marriage, and Family

Relationship with God

W ho is generally the first person superstars thank when receiving an award? Well, you are right if you guessed God. Even though people who live a lifestyle that is in extreme contradiction to the person they profess gave them the talent to acquire such notoriety; they still have an awareness of His hand on their success. God has been and will always be the big elephant in the room as it pertains to the affairs of mankind. So his relationship with us is worthy of mention.

First and foremost, men and women (of all ages) are dependent on God. If He were to snap his fingers, He could instantly remove the breath of every living organism on the face of the planet. We depend on the one who created us. There is no such thing as life without God, contrary to popular belief. We derive our sense of purpose, identity and value from God. There are other little bells and whistles that give us a sense of these aforementioned concepts too, but the source of them lies in God alone.

I've made it pretty clear in this book so far that God created man. He also desires a real relationship with his creation. The 66 books of the bible are a huge romance novel detailing the efforts of a loving God wanting to walk alongside the people he created. Simply put, God is crazy about you and me. There is nothing that he will not sacrifice in order to make sure that we have a strong and healthy relationship with Him, which He demonstrated through the sacrifice of His only begotten Son, Jesus Christ. This relationship is vital to us because without it we can do nothing of lasting value. Anything that we do manage to pull off on our own is just God being gracious to us until we wise up and realize how much we need Him.

God is like a great filmmaker. He has a script that He has created for each and every one of our lives. In this script, He has a clear way that He wants things to flow and develop for us. Yet He gives us the choice to play our assigned roles or not. We can only understand this role and the parts of the script that we need to know by staying in close proximity to him. It sounds very basic, but we live in a world that makes it hard to remember this principle.

Relationship with God has to be cultivated and developed like any other one; however, it is the most important. It takes effort on our part to ensure that we are in step with God. He will never force us to be in a relationship with Him even though He yearns for it. God will sometimes let some of us see how messed up our lives can become without Him. Often times, this causes us to turn to Him for a better life. Yet others refuse to be in relationship with God at their own peril and some even blame God for their own bad decisions.

God has the ultimate perspective on all things. He knows every situation we will ever face. It is to our own benefit to place our full confidence in him because he knows how things are going to turn out. He's the only one who truly has the power to change things that are outside of our control. God is the only being that can truly sustain our hearts when we go through extreme setbacks and trouble. Have you ever been through an ordeal so difficult that you could not even articulate the pain you were in? I have. I've been in places so low that even when I tried to communicate how I was feeling to others they just didn't get it. I didn't "get it" myself sometimes due to the severity of what I was facing. One of the most amazing qualities about God is that He understands us when no one else does. One of the greatest components of a relationship is the ability for two individuals to have an ongoing understanding of one another. A chief desire in every heart is to be understood.

Nobody understands us to the depth that God does. He is the only person big enough to accept all of our flaws, joys and everything in between. One of the qualities that I love most about God is that He is able to absorb all of me and everything I feel, good or bad. There is no one else who has the propensity to do that at the level that the human soul needs.

God Orders Our Life Steps

As I mentioned a little earlier, God has designed the script of our lives. I love the passage found in Ephesians 2:10 that states, "For we are God's workmanship, created in Christ Jesus to do good works, which God prepared in advance for us to do." There are good works and accomplishments that have our name on it. Therefore, we have no need to try to force things in our lives. If we stay close to God, we will walk through every door that He purposed for us.

I used to ask God to open up windows of opportunity, but now I often find myself requesting that He order my steps. I have learned that there is a huge difference in the value of these two requests. We may be presented with opportunities that may not be the right ones or that we may not be prepared to handle. Our recognition of this depends on what the condition of our hearts is. I have found that when my heart is desperate and discontent, it is easy for me to fall prey to seemingly good opportunities that will later ensnare me. If I have spent adequate time in God's presence, my heart is more at rest and I trust that God's path for me is right, no matter what it looks like on the surface. During those moments, it is easier for me to accept God's plan and let him order my steps.

God is always thousands of steps ahead of us, so it pays to just follow him. The opportunities that appear to be good today have a very harsh reality attached to them later on down the road. We are unable to see into the future, but God does because he dwells in eternity. He is not bound by the laws of time as man is. He knows what the result of something will be way before it is conceptualized in the heart of a human. Situations that appear to be losses often will result in our greatest triumphs if we will trust God as He leads us through them.

I remember a time when there was a very attractive promotion slotted for me in a brand-new division of the company that I worked for at the time. They paid for all of my training and expenses in order to groom me for this impressive position in mid-level management. As a kid in my early twenties at the time, this would've been a huge leap for me. Once I completed my training, I expected to move immediately into this new position. But instead I had to face the uncertainty of management and it appeared that I possibly wasn't getting the position after all. I was so distraught and began to get depressed. Here I was in my early twenties with a chance to move up the corporate ladder but internal politics was keeping me from progressing. I prayed to God and also consulted with my mentor. Then I finally got to a point where I just told God to have His way. I wasn't going to fight for this position any longer. To be quite honest, I was out of energy and emotional stamina anyway.

It turned out that I did not get that promotion. At first I was very upset. But then after a while, God began to reveal to me the problems that I would have faced had I received the position. It turns out that the senior managers within this new division were totally unorganized but too prideful to admit it. The senior-level manager and the middle manager (the position I would have had) constantly bumped heads and tension resulted in several meltdowns within that division. Had I been in that position, it would have brought incredible stress and heartache into my life that I may not have been ready to handle.

On the flipside, I did end up getting promoted within another division of the company that was under more stable senior management. What's more, I was promoted twice within one year and did very well in both positions. While all of this good was happening in my life, I had a front-row seat at the demise of the other division that God rescued me from. God saw way beyond the temporary yearning of my ego and envisioned the best outcome for my life. I ended up obtaining invaluable skill sets and experience that serve me well to this day.

God's plans for our lives are always maximized beyond what we can ask, think or imagine. All I could see was a promotion. God saw two promotions, less stress, more money, professional experience, character building and the development of transferable skills. The part that frustrates me at times about letting God order my steps is that He generally takes me the long way. He is more concerned about who we become during the journey than getting us to a particular destination. The true treasure is found in the journey. As I mature, I increasingly come to appreciate God's scenic routes instead of the shortcuts.

Our Relationship with God Determines the Quality of Our Relationships with Others

When we are in right relationship with God it makes it a little easier to relate to others. The awareness of God's unconditional love allows us to demonstrate this same type of love to people. God's higher perspective radically transforms our lowly ones helping us to see beyond ourselves. When we can view life beyond ourselves then we are able to be empathetic to the needs of those around us. Empathy is one of the core derivatives of emotional intelligence.

Emotional intelligence is a byproduct of a strong connection with God. I find that I am a much better husband to my wife when I get the necessary relational nutrients from my heavenly Father. God fills us up so we can pour Him out. Even the most educated emotional health specialists are not able to relate to people in the most accurate way without God's presence on their lives.

Relationship with God gives us the confidence that is necessary to overcome the fear found in bonding with others. I don't know about you, but sometimes I get afraid when I become attached to people because it puts me in a vulnerable position. I once heard a wise person say, "You can only be hurt by people that you care about." Another wise person remarked, "The truth is, everyone will hurt you, you just have to determine who is worth suffering for." With that said, relying on God's love enables us to get beyond our fears of being hurt and engage in the scary act of loving people. According to 1 John 4:18, "There is no fear in love. But perfect love casts out all fear…" Since God is love (1 John 4:8), a life filled with God will cause you and I to eventually become fearless. The closer we get to God, the more we will be able to overcome the relational fears that we have (and any other fears for that matter). Forming deep relationships with other people is one of the most frightening things to do. We risk being rejected, disappointed and abandoned by people even when we do right by them. Many people can't overcome the hurt caused by people and decide to isolate themselves or wear a mask that protects them from outsiders. Neither of these options leads to accuracy.

> *Nobody understands us to the depth that God does. He is the only person big enough to accept all of our flaws, our joys, and everything in between.*

Therefore, we have to learn how to rely on God. That is the only way to relate to others despite the deep wounds in our souls that we have both inflicted and received. I should mention here that God has other resources that He uses that make it possible for us to connect properly with others. These can include life coaches, psychologists, relationship books and seminars. But God is the ultimate source of our relational capacity. Relating to God in a healthy manner lays the proper foundation needed to reach out to others.

How to Relate to God

There are four primary ways that I have found that allow me to connect with God. You may be able to add more to the list, these are just the foundational ones for me. These are prayer, worship, study and obedience. There are other ancillary ways of communing with God, but even most of those fall into one of these four categories.

Prayer

There is much discussion and commentary on what prayer is. One basic definition is that it is communication with God. To take that thought further, it is communication with God that causes us to exchange our thoughts, wants, and desires for His. Prayer is not a one-way conversation, it is a bilateral one. We should pray with the expectation that God will communicate back. It is true that prayer changes things, but it more so changes us. Once we are changed, we are empowered to change our environments and circumstances. God takes care of the stuff that is out of our control. But I am often surprised by how things shift in my world when I allow God to change my thoughts, beliefs and attitudes.

When I pray, I can sense when God is communicating back to me. It isn't necessarily an audible voice, but it is a clear distinct message that I receive internally. Sometimes God will give me a vision of something I need to do or I am reminded of a passage of scripture that I read at one point that is now relevant for my current situation. Prayer also makes me more aware of God's presence in my life. He is there whether I am conscious of Him or not. But there is a drastic change in how I approach life when I know He is with me. Things that worry me or seem insurmountable began to shrink in comparison to a big God who is crazy about me and who would do anything to ensure my well-being.

I'm starting to get into the habit of writing down my concerns, problems and desires in a journal before I pray so that I can get them out of my mind. I then begin to pray and thank God for his goodness.

Once I feel that I have made a secure connection with God (sort of like Wi-Fi) I then begin to discuss with Him the issues that I wrote down on the paper. One reason I like doing it like this is that when I begin to pray, God then starts to give me his perspective on my life. He shows me how I should even view the concerns that I wrote down. When I begin to talk with Him about my problems and/or desires, I am speaking with Him from a higher perspective than I originally began with. My perspective is more like His than my own (even though much of my own human perspective is intertwined). There is a glorious freedom I have found in praying to God in such a way. It allows for me to communicate with Him effectively because I am speaking with Him from an authentic standpoint, rather than just out of religious obligation.

Prayer can be a difficult habit to form. Even though I have witnessed the power of it several times and the difference it makes, busyness and my own pride get in the way. For one, it is hard to communicate to someone who is unseen. It can feel foolish at times, especially if you don't do it on a regular basis. God has graciously shown himself to be real in my life so many times that I cannot deny his existence or His power. So sometimes I am faced with the dilemma of knowing too much about God to not believe in prayer, but too worried about taking care of myself that I try to take matters into my own hands without consulting with Him first.

The only way to really grow in your awareness of God is to cultivate a consistent prayer life. Perhaps you can start with a small amount of time, like 10 or 15 minutes a day and then gradually increase it when you gain the discipline to do so. I am at a point now that I feel naked and vulnerable when I have not prayed. God has shown me how much I depend on Him for everything. Prayer allows us to connect with God's thoughts and will. There is no higher level of thought than that of God's.

Worship

Worship means to prostrate oneself in the presence of a greater person. It is an act of both internal and external homage. I find myself in seasons of life where I literally bow down and sing to God and profess His goodness, others were I sit quietly and just reflect on His greatness. He is pleased with both if we are sincere. Worship is one of the most spiritual things we can do. In fact, spiritual worship is the only type of worship that God accepts and desires.

This may sound crazy, but we have to allow God within us to worship God that is outside of us. Let me explain. God has given us His Spirit, if we have come to place our trust in Jesus, His Son. The Spirit that lives in us is one in the same as God in Heaven. The Spirit that He gave us is the only one qualified to worship God because they are both the same substance (Spirit). God's Spirit connects with our human spirit, allowing us to have fellowship with Him. It also worth mentioning that the Spirit of God living within us helps us accurately pray to God. There is a human aspect to my worship, which is my willingness to get out of the way and let the Spirit of God sync up with God. Once I get self out of the way, God has free access to the Spirit of God within me. It's very powerful when this transaction takes place.

Worship is the product of intimacy. God desires to have a deep relationship with each and every one of us. We are able to touch God's heart through worship and He is able to touch ours. People have the innate inclination to worship, but it's just a matter of whom or what they will give that honor to. The only person worthy of our worship is the One who created us. We have to guard against worshipping anyone or anything besides God.

Study

We gain accurate knowledge of God by studying the Holy Bible. The Bible is the mind of God in tangible form. It is the most powerful book on the planet. I remember watching the movie, *The Book of Eli*. In it, the villain was passionately after the last copy of the Bible which Eli, portrayed by Denzel Washington, had. In this film, the Bible was considered the most powerful weapon in post-apocalyptic America and people were willing to die to obtain it. This movie painted a beautiful illustration of how valuable the Word of God is.

There is power contained in it that no power can match. God's Word states that "God's foolishness is greater than man's wisdom." Wow! How crazy is that? The best man has to offer doesn't come close to the worst God has. The Bible is not just another book — it is the book that is essential to living accurately. It covers the entire gamut of human existence. The Word of God discusses everything from business to romance. The Bible can show you how to run a Fortune 500 company and how to raise children. There isn't a more complete book on the market.

One of the main reasons it's important to study the Word of God is because it is an anchor for our minds. There is a lot of crazy information that floats around and we all need something to keep us grounded to the truth. If we were to give our minds to everything we saw or read without having a point of centrality, there would be no stability in our lives. Stability is crucial to sustainable growth and expansion. That need is met through God's Word. Truth be told, there is probably no other book you would ever need to read if you were just left with the Bible. I am grateful for other works and authors, but the Bible is the ultimate source for information.

Obedience

We come to know God better as we are obedient to His voice. God speaks in a variety of ways. I personally hear clearest from God by reading His Word and through prayer. I also get little nudges here and there throughout the day when I need to make decisions. God is constantly speaking to those who want to listen to His direction. He provides guidance for our lives in real time. It is up to us to respond properly to His instructions by doing what He says when He says it. If we are obedient to his voice, we will find that we will be much better off in life. The things that He tells us to do may not always make sense to us at that moment, but we will reap the benefits of it later.

God has told me to call people at a time that seemed random to me. But when I called them, I came to find out that they really needed to talk and they ended up not making a decision that could have shipwrecked their life. There have been other times where God told me not to enter into certain business relationships with people who appeared to be important to my advancement. He later revealed that these business partnerships would have resulted in financial loss, heart ache, stress and hindered progression.

> *God is the designer of our lives and He knows each step we need to take to reach the goals He has set for us.*

His direction can often appear illogical to the human mind. That is because His insight is so much greater than ours; God views our lives from a comprehensive vantage point. We are advised not to trust our own human understanding, but to consult with God in all things. Our sight is extremely limited and many times we make decisions based on emotions and past experiences, which can be very inaccurate. God is the designer of our lives and He knows each step we need to take to reach the goals he has set for us.

We will become increasingly accurate in understanding God's voice and His will for our lives as we learn to be obedient to Him. We will find that God will reveal more of His eternal reality to those who don't try to hold on to our temporary reality. Many people can't trust God because they can't loosen the grip that they have on their life. Obedience to God leads to greater peace and stability. Even if all kinds of crazy circumstances are breaking out against you, many blessings will follow your obedience to His voice.

Marriage

Simply put, marriage is the second-most sacred, beautiful and intimate relationship you will ever have, after the one you have with God. In my own experience, the richest moments in my life have been shared with my wife. I've done some cool things on my own but those same things possess an even greater level of satisfaction when enjoyed with my wife, Menzelle. On the flipside, I've gone through some of my darkest seasons of life and my wife has helped me through them with her love, support and prayers. It is truly a blessing to have someone in your life that can experience all of it with you.

With that said, marriage takes a lot of work. It takes time, energy and emotional investment. Marriage also requires sacrifice, selflessness and grace. My wife and I have had our good times, bad times and just plain boring times too. This all comes with marriage and we must embrace all of it in order to have a healthy and long-lasting union.

Have you ever wondered why more than 50 percent of marriages end in divorce? I have and it's a topic that I continue to contemplate because I don't want to fall into this statistic. I'm fortunate enough to have seen both the ugly and beautiful side of marriage. I've seen couples married for longer than 60 years, like my grandparents, and others who divorced after three short months. Every marriage is different, but there are some key components that lead to greater accuracy and longevity. Remaining married, better yet happily married, will take work my friend. It will not just happen.

Perseverance

I read an inspiring article about Herbert and Zelmyra Fisher, who, at the time, held the record for the longest marriage in the world. They had been married for 86 years, until Herbert passed away at age 105 in 2011. Together, they lived through World War II, the Korean War, the Vietnam War and saw the first man land on the moon. Most people these days can't sit through a whole movie let alone spend their lives in a faithful relationship with a single spouse. Though the Fishers said that there really was no secret to a lasting marriage, other than God, they did state perseverance was a key characteristic that helped them do it. They stated in a 2012 interview with The Stir that "you have to be willing to stick it out." For them divorce was never an option — or even a thought.

The Fishers determined to hang in through the rough patches in marriage that are inevitable. Today, we are quick to file for divorce at the first signs of difficulty. That mindset does not work in marriage. Storms have to be weathered and once they are, a marriage becomes stronger as a result. My wife and I look back on some of the hardships we have faced with thankfulness because it caused us to become closer. Our relationship has a greater depth because of the trouble we have overcome together. That type of closeness cannot be produced in any other way.

> *One of the biggest mistakes we can make is to give up on our marriage when times are rocky.*

One of the biggest mistakes we can make is to give up on our marriage when times are rocky. We rob ourselves of developing an even stronger bond when we throw in the towel. I have seen the benefits of persevering through problems in my own marriage. God has an interesting way of repairing and fortifying relationships that have endured the pain of human imperfection. Marriage is the union of two imperfect people committing to a life of fidelity and unity before God. You can imagine that there are going to be issues with this type of arrangement. But those who stick it out, like the Fishers, reap huge rewards physically, emotionally and spiritually.

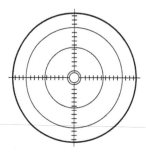

Scope of Accuracy – Herbert and Zelmyra Fisher

Herbert and Zelmyra Fisher got married on May 13, 1924. They really lived up to the promise of staying together until "death do you part." The humble couple, who grew up in James City, North Carolina, lived in the home that Herbert built with his bare hands in 1942. Zelmyra said her husband was "quiet and kind." Herbert responded by saying that she never gave him "no trouble." Neither of them expected to be married so long, but they both agreed that divorce was not an option. They lived together through the Great Depression, the Civil Rights Movement and 15 presidential administrations. Though they were poor, they managed to save enough money to put all five of their children through college. Herbert died at 105 in 2011 and Zelmyra joined her husband in 2013, when she passed away at the same age.

Communication

I have learned that communication involves much more than just talking to someone. It involves listening intently with both empathy and logic in order to get a true understanding of what the other person is saying. Effective communicators are able to hear the message within the words being spoken to them. They are able figure out the underlying meaning couched within the actions of others. It takes deep communication to have a healthy marriage.

One of my favorite books on the subject of relationships is *The 5 Love Languages* by Dr. Gary Chapman. He asserts that each person has a different way that they are able to acknowledge and receive love. It is the job of each spouse to discover the love language that clicks with their partner. Once this happens, our spouses will be more fulfilled in the relationship. We run into trouble when we try to communicate love in a way that isn't how our spouse is wired to receive it. Both the sender and receiver in the communication wind up frustrated because neither party is obtaining the results they expected from the transaction.

For example, the way my wife is wired to receive love is by me spending time with her. The amount of money I spend on her is not the highest expression of love for her because that is not her primary love language. It took me several years to understand this and we bumped heads a lot initially because I didn't know how to communicate love the way she needed it. And I'm still learning!

Every person is complex with unique view points, backgrounds, desires, emotions, passions, goals and ambitions. I am sometimes bewildered when reminded that I'm married to another human being that has as many layers as me that comprises who she is. It is easy to take people you're around consistently for granted. I am both humbled and excited by the fact that I will have a lifetime to discover more about my wife and how to communicate with her.

Communication is the lifeblood of relationships. There is no way to know someone without communicating with them on a regular basis. Many marriages fail because they lack healthy dialogue. I love what Stephen R. Covey states in his book, *The 7 Habits of Highly Effective People*: We must first seek to understand, then to be understood. People often seek to be understood first and then try to understand later, if at all. An accurate transmission of ideas will suffer if one or both parties are already forming a response in their mind while the other is still relaying information. We wouldn't have to talk as much if we took the time to fully listen and appreciate what people are conveying to us. This would lead to less arguments, misunderstandings and problem in our relationships.

In marriage, we must go the extra mile and put our need to get our point across on the backburner (even if we feel we are right). Our spouses must know that we value their outlook and we do this by respectfully absorbing the information they disseminate to us. For husbands, this may mean simply letting our wives vent and not trying to solve their problems (which we men often rush to do). For wives, this may be displayed by giving a non-critical ear to your husband's ideas, no matter how whimsical they may sound. At the end of the day, people just want to know that their voices are heard and valued. This is especially true in a marriage.

Sacrifice

An accurate marriage comes at a price. That price is often one of giving up the right to only consider your well-being. Before we speak, we have to consider the impact that our words will have on our spouses, even if what we're saying is true. We have to give thought about how our actions and decisions will impact our partner, even if the results are positive for us (as individuals). You're no longer a single entity once you cross the threshold of marriage. You must learn how to operate as a unit. It's no longer "I," only "us."

A vast amount of married couples find themselves in a doomed relationship because they fail to make the transition from "me" to "we." It's natural to fall into this trap. Most of us have been raised to be individualistic and we take this same mindset into marriage. We have to let go of our individualistic mentality, and this is not an easy process. It is a slow proression we endure each day. Sacrifice always means loss. You often gain a greater benefit when you sacrifice in marriage, but it is not always immediate and it is still painful, nonetheless.

Sometimes we have to even sacrifice dreams, aspirations and fulfilling activities once we get married that were under our individualistic paradigm. We now must include our spouses on these same ambitions or visions and allow them the time to get comfortable with our aspirations. This can be incredibly hard to do and even irritating. But we will discover that there will be much more harmony in our unions and even greater momentum available for the things we envision if we are willing to sacrifice going after them as if we were still single.

Successful marriages often include compromises and negotiations. I hate to use business terms to discuss marriage, but we are often engaged in selling and deal brokering in our partnerships. We try to create win-win situations in our household because we feel that neither partner should feel taken advantage of. In certain seasons though, you may have to give 70 percent while your spouse is only able to give 30 percent. Sometimes love is painful and you must be willing to pay the price in order to keep the marriage alive.

Mature people are able to sacrifice for the greater good. I think a lot of people don't understand that marriage is a mature person's sport. Maturity allows a person to take their eyes off of self and focus on the welfare of others. It's tempting to be selfish, especially in today's society. People often get married for self-fulfilling reasons. Marriage and selfishness will never mix. Those who try to force these opposites together end up in a living hell.

Patience

You've probably heard the saying "patience is a virtue." Well, I'm here to tell you that it is an absolute necessity in marriage. As I mentioned a little earlier, marriage is the union of two imperfect people committing to a

> *The fact that every human being has flaws and imperfections means that there has to be a greater amount of forgiveness extended in marriage.*

life of fidelity and oneness before God. The fact that every human being has flaws and imperfections means that there has to be a greater amount of forgiveness extended in marriage. The head-over-heels sensation that new love produces will not last forever. During this period of time, we are able to overlook (sometimes to our own detriment) the issues that our potential spouse has. Once the love magic wears off, we are left with the bad breath, dirty dishes, filthy laundry, irritating laughs, symphony-style snoring and other irritants without the new love drug to cover all this.

Patience plays a huge role in marriage; we must acknowledge that we have traits that are just as irksome to our spouse, if not more. We do things that are normal by our standards, but excruciatingly aggravating to the person we share the bed with. Understanding this reality should cause us to ease up a little bit on our partner. It's not to suggest that we let everything slide, but we are to be graceful with one another's imperfections.

We have to allow room for non-fatal mistakes and error in marriage. They are bound to happen between people who possess gaps (which everyone has). A sure way to kill your marriage is to be rigid and unforgiving when your spouse makes a bad judgment call, especially those not intentionally meant to hurt you. Sometimes people don't even realize the mistakes they are making because they have never been pointed out before. What you consider a misstep or offensive may come as a complete surprise to your spouse because it wasn't a big deal when they were single.

Once you get married and thereafter, remind yourself often that both you and your spouse have entirely different backgrounds. There are disparate expectations, norms, traditions and value systems that both parties bring to the relationship. It takes times for these contrary paradigms to sync up and form a new one that will encompass elements of both. Even after this new paradigm is established, remnants of the old paradigms will resurface from time to time.

Furthermore, there may be some differences that are never really resolved and smoothed over. Sometimes both people just have to accept certain aspects of one another. In due time, you may come to appreciate your differences as you discover that they fill in some of the gaps that you have as an individual. Sadly, many couples give up on their union before they come to realize the benefits of their differences. True, there may be some idiosyncrasies that your spouse has that you can do without, but if you dig deeper, you will see that the hidden treasure outweighs the bad.

Romance

Romance is one of the most tremendous aspects of marriage. Romance is not just making love. Love-making is actually just the by-product of romance. Popular culture speaks of dating and courtship as if they were only appropriate during singlehood. The truth is, dating and courtship should continue after we are married as well. Your romantic life should actually increase once you tie the knot. It takes more creativity to stay captivated by the love of a spouse than it does for a non-exclusive partner. Therefore, romance plays a huge role in having a healthy marriage.

> *There should be times that you don't even engage in sex, but set a romantic climate in the home that will eventually lead up to that.*

We guys have a bad habit of just trying to have sex with our wives and putting no effort into setting the atmosphere for them. I am guilty of this in my own marriage. Romance is just as much about the little things as it is the big ones. You would be surprised how far holding hands, writing little love notes and surprise foot massages go in a marriage. There should be times that you don't even engage in sex, but set a romantic climate in the home that will eventually lead up to that. An accurate marriage has an environment that encourages intimacy.

Find out what your spouse enjoys and what makes them feel sexy. Again, it is not just about sex, but it is about brining pleasure to your partner both mentally and physically. Get into the habit of complimenting your spouse on things that they do well and the aspects of their appearance that you really appreciate. Give hugs and kisses often. My wife and I have gotten in the habit of always kissing each other before we leave each other's presence for any length of time. Things like that strengthen our connection and promote a loving experience in our union.

It is good to designate one day of the week as date night. This day (or night) is reserved for you and your spouse to spend concentrated time together alone. You cannot schedule any meetings or have any friends over during this time. Another thing, cell phones, computers and tablets must be turned off. How scary is that? Most couples these days can't take their eyes off of their electronic devices. The demands of married life don't make it easy to maintain healthy romance. So this is something we have to fight to keep.

Marriages are especially susceptible to attack in the area of romance. Popular media generally portrays married life as a death sentence or a fantasy world. It is not common to see romantically vibrant marriages in mainstream entertainment. Therefore, we must be cautious about what we feed ourselves because that will come to be our reality eventually. Read books and watch visual content that promotes a healthy love life in your home.

Prayer and Spiritual Union

Cultivating a collective relationship with God is essential to an accurate marriage. God is the one who ordained marriage and it is regarded as the most sacred human covenant on earth. Therefore, God must be the foundation for our marriages. It is crucial for married couples to pray and seek the face of God together often. It is good for both partners to engage God personally, but there is an even greater force released when a husband and wife do so together.

Believe it or not, the current world order is very much opposed to marriage. We live in a world that seeks to operate without God's involvement. Marriage between man and wife is symbolic of Jesus Christ's relationship with the church. There are powers and authorities that are very offended and afraid of the power of this union. Human marriages are a symbol to spiritual powers in opposition to God. Therefore, it is attacked vigorously.

When you marry someone, a target is placed on your back. The success of your marriage is a threat to the paradigm that opposes God. Combine spiritual warfare with your own personal imperfections and it can be a recipe for disaster. So it takes the power of God to keep a marriage together. It is absolute foolishness to try to be married without God's covering. There are many godless marriages, but they are littered with all types of dysfunction. Even God-filled marriages have their mountains of trouble, so you can imagine how much harder it is to be married without being connected to God.

One of my most favorite parts of marriage is that I have someone who I know will pray for me if I ask it of them. My wife and I worship God together. We are incredibly excited about pursuing God and being a part of His will as a unit.

Love Bank Accounts

I've read many books on marriage and several of them have made mention of a concept called the love bank. The idea behind it is that love is similar to a bank account, and withdrawals and deposits are constantly being made. If too many withdrawals are made, your marriage is in danger and desperately needs some love deposits. A love bank with a high balance is very healthy and can survive some withdrawals here and there.

Withdrawals are those actions that may hurt you or your spouse. These take away from good feelings and thoughts that you have toward one another. On the other hand, deposits are activities that make you or your spouse feel good and promote loving thoughts toward one another. It should be regular practice for married couples to make deposits into their love banks because there are definitely going to be some withdrawals. The goal is to get your love bank to a level where it can survive huge withdrawals after they happen. It takes more effort to make a love deposit than a withdrawal, so spouses must be intentional about building the account.

A former colleague of mine once told me that you have to get into the habit of doing sweet things for your spouse "just because." There shouldn't have to be any special holiday or reason why you go out and do something kind for your partner. Buy her some flowers or cook him a nice dinner just because. This is one of the surest ways to build the love bank up. It is easier to let offenses slide if there have been successive quality deposits made.

A lot of married couples wait until they are in trouble before they start trying to rectify the relationship. Get a head start on the stormy seasons by demonstrating random love to your spouse. The great thing about some bank accounts is that they also can accrue interests if you leave a certain amount of money in them. Love is the same way: If you keep a high balance, you are much more likely to see offshoots of that love pop up spontaneously and without much additional effort on your part.

My wife and I have had our rough patches, much like any marriage does. But when it is good between us, it is great. It is a beautiful thing to enjoy going home and being with your spouse. I want to now pause our discussion on marriage and transition into family relationships.

Family

> *We must persevere in becoming better family members and be patient with others who are not as committed to the process as we are.*

The way that we relate to our family will change depending on what season of life we are in. It's far too broad a topic to fully expound upon in this short section, but I'll just give some basic principles that are a good place to start. Let me start by saying that family is very important. As we have become more individualistic as a society, modern culture has gotten away from this crucial bond. Family relationships are being redefined and not for the better. There is less honor and respect shown toward parents and less support and structure provided for children. It will take a conscious effort on the part of those desiring to live a life of accuracy to make sure that their homes are moving in the right direction.

I am merely a passionate researcher seeking to discover and implement what is accurate. My family is not perfect by any stretch of the imagination; honestly, there is no perfect family. Each home has its fair share of dysfunction.

Our goal as family members should be to always improve our relationships and deepen our bonds with each other in healthy ways. These changes won't happen if we don't make the effort. It will take intentionality, prayer, and guidance. We must persevere in becoming better family members and be patient with others who are not as committed to the process as we are. If we practice persistence, we will have a shot at motivating the other family members to follow suit.

A Lesson from the Huxtables

If you were born in the '80s, you may remember the television program, *The Cosby Show*. In my opinion, this was one of the greatest television shows ever produced. Bill Cosby and company kept me and my family rolling on the ground from laughter. There was also some sort of lesson or gem of wisdom that was given on most of the shows as well. What I began to appreciate later on in my life about this show was the family values that it modeled. It provided an example of what family life could look like for me and my peers.

You had a husband and a wife who were very much in love with each other, committed to their union and to their children. They were educated, hardworking and striving to help their kids obtain a great future. The beauty in this show was that though this was probably not the reality for many of my peers and I growing up, it created an ideal for us that didn't seem too farfetched. Clair and Cliff Huxtable (portrayed by Phylicia Rashad and Cosby) seemed so believable and natural as a couple on the show that I often wondered if they were married in real life (they were not). You almost got the sense that the cast of the show was a real family. To this day, I respect and even try to emulate the ideals that this show presented in my own home. There are no lights, cameras or studio audience in my real life, but that doesn't mean that value derived from a television show can't be transferred into it. The Huxtables represented to me what could be, with my own twist of reality mixed in, of course.

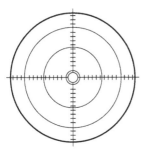

Scope of Accuracy – Bill Cosby

William Henry Cosby Jr., better known as Bill Cosby, is one of the most iconic entertainers of all time. He is best known for his mega sitcom hit "The Cosby Show," which was based on an affluent, upper middle class, African-American family living in Brooklyn Heights, New York. Cosby has transcended racial and generational boundaries, and is affectionately known as "America's dad." "The Cosby Show" is one of only three American programs that have been No. 1 in the Nielsen ratings for at least five consecutive seasons. It is well noted that Cosby's sitcom saved NBC during a time when the network's ratings were extremely low. Before his success with "The Cosby Show," his role in the popular 1960s TV show "I Spy" made him the first African-American to co-star in a dramatic series. Cosby broke television's racial barrier and won three Emmy Awards.

In addition, Cosby has earned eight gold records, five platinum records, and five Grammys for his comedy albums. He has been married to his lovely wife, Camille, for more than 50 years and is a father of five children. His son, Ennis, was tragically killed in a shooting in Los Angeles while changing a tire. Even after times of hardship and controversy, Cosby has emerged as one of the most successful people in America and is a mainstay in the hearts of the masses.

We all need an goal to work toward. As I stated earlier, everything starts from a vision. It is important to have a vision for what your family should look like. If you can conceptualize it, then there is a greater possibility of making it tangible. For me, the Huxtables (along with "real families") have helped shaped what I envision for my family relationships.

For the Rest of Us

Though there is no such thing as the perfect family, we should all strive to have great and emotionally healthy families. It is the responsibility of each member to contribute to the family unit, even if they are under age. It is easy to take the members of your family for granted because you see them often and that may cause you to devalue them.

Some people have been extremely hurt by family and this can create an environment of disrespect and sometimes outright hate. We have to recognize where hurt has been caused, learn how to process through the pain, and chose to see the good in our family members, even if it's not glaringly apparent. It can be especially hard to do this if the family member that hurt us never apologizes for their past actions. Yet, to stay on the track of accuracy, we must learn how to forgive and move on. I have also learned that many people don't intentionally mean the harm that they cause us; they just don't know any better, especially if they've been hurt in the same way. This is not to excuse harmful behavior, but it helps us develop a culture of deeper understanding and forgiveness within our homes.

I once heard the life story of NBA star Dwayne Wade, who had a hard childhood. His mother was a drug addict and dealer for most of his young life and he witnessed many horrible things as a kid. She was even sentenced to prison for drug charges when Wade was in high school and college. Wade and his sister would watch his mom shoot dope in her arm and they were forced to be around other drug addicts on a regular basis. She eventually got clean and became a born-again Christian. The most amazing part of this story is that Wade never held it against her. When you see them together, it's as if that season of pain never even occurred in their lives. Wade even went on to buy his mom (now a pastor) and her congregation a $2 million building to hold services in. She attends all of his games and she is a very happy mother and grandmother today. Wade still honors his mother despite her dark past and they have moved on to have a healthy mother-son relationship.

We all have dark chasms to cross because of our imperfect humanity. The place where this is seen in its ugliest form is in the family environment. Our family members see sides of us that would ruin our reputation if the outside world caught a glimpse. And on the flipside, we see the ugliest parts of our loved ones. Yet, I have learned that this provides a tremendous opportunity to show true honor to our family members. It is harder to honor someone when you see their faults. But if you can choose to overlook the bad and honor them in spite, this is true reverence. The same goes for practicing love. True love has its greatest expression during times when people are unlovable. Conflict tests the mettle of any relationship.

It is in these challenging moments where the capacity to love and honor can be increased. Loving and honoring our families when it hurts will develop an endurance in us that is not seen in our current culture anymore. This endurance will help turn the tide of a culture who gives up on anything and anyone that cause them two seconds of displeasure. Our families must get back to this commitment so that the family doesn't deteriorate.

Communication Filters

To center our discussion on communication filters in families, I'll start it off with a somewhat comical story. There was a very small man who was the size of a 3-year-old toddler. However, this man happened to be in his mid-40s. Every day of his adult life he had to deal with people trying to either pick him up or rescue him because they thought he was a stranded child. Even when people heard his deep voice, they still refused to believe he was a grown up. What made it worse is he also had a smoking and drinking habit, so you can imagine how this looked to outsiders. When he finally landed a decent job, he had to endure his bosses talking to him like a child rather than an educated and informed adult.

Day in and day out he worked hard to perform his duties at a high level and often went above and beyond what was required of him. Even still, he was laughed at and mocked by his peers. Hardly anyone showed him the respect that he deserved. No one could see past his physical appearance and acknowledge the highly intelligent and mature professional that he really was. He never received a promotion at work or any other organization that he belonged to because people could only see his size and not his character.

Our families often fall into the same boat as this person in my fictional story. You see it especially with parents and children. Some parents never allow their children to grow up even after these children have families of their own. As a result, some children still expect to be babied even when they are adults and capable of taking care of themselves. We often have the tendency of communicating to our perceptions of people rather than who people really are. Much like the child-sized man was treated, we can communicate to a grown person as if he or she is a child. Siblings, aunts, uncles, nieces and nephews all do this to one another. It is always interesting to me to see how people act once they get back into their family settings. A person may be a power executive of a Fortune 500 company, but once they get to their mother's house, they fall back into the role of spoiled brat or family peacemaker. You'll even find the parents communicating to this power executive as if he were still a pimple-faced teenager. I understand that children will always be children to their parents, but families have to learn how to allow one another to evolve and mature, not only physically but mentally.

> *True love has its greatest expression during times when people are unlovable. Conflict tests the mettle of any relationship.*

Families should grow together. Oftentimes, this does not happen. A healthy thing is a growing thing and the same is true of families. We should not only grow numerically and in material possessions, but we should collectively be growing mentally, spiritually and relationally. If this occurred, we would see less dysfunction in our families. Our communication filters play a huge role in our family development. First we must recognize when we are communicating from an inaccurate filter (most times we are). Secondly, we must assess how the family member we are speaking to has matured. This will require us to do less talking and more listening. Thirdly, we then need to acknowledge and affirm this change in our family members when communicating. If we make these adjustments, we will see more harmony and togetherness in our family units.

You would be surprised at what two minutes of displayed respect can do in even the most hostile of relationships. If we chose to put our biases and previous judgments of family members on the back burner and decided to hear them out, we can spark instant growth. I remember having a conversation about life with my older sister a while ago. My sister and I clearly have some serious communication filter issues, to the point where it is sometimes hard to take one another serious because we joke so much. We often fall into a tirade of playfulness because that is pretty much how we have been our whole lives. But this time, during this specific conversation, I was determined for it to go another direction. We hadn't seen each other for some time and I really wanted to hear how life had been for her. I listened intently and didn't give any feedback while she spoke. I knew that if I had done that, it may have discouraged her from opening up and sharing what was really in her heart. We ended up having a great conversation and I was able to hear how she had grown because I gave her room to express that. I'm not patting myself on the back, but I was able to discover an underlying principle in this accurate decision that I made.

For an instant, I took off my younger sibling hat, and listened to my sister speak as if we were both two mature adults (which we are) and I was able to gain greater access into her world. For so long, I had been an outsider just making wild guesses and inaccurate assessments of the woman my sister was becoming because I was communicating through an old filter. We have to get to a place where we allow our family members the space to be who they truly are, instead of placing on them the limitations and unfair double standards that we have created. Again, many of us are unaware that we do this, so we have to become conscience of our communication filters.

Application of Accuracy

God

- **Realize that you are dependent on God for everything.**
- **Your relationship with God has to be cultivated, developed and maintained.**
- **We relate to God through prayer, worship, study of His Word, obedience and the difficulties we endure in life.**

Marriage

- **Love is not enough. Marital longevity requires perseverance and commitment.**
- **Marriage is about sacrifice and patience. You and your spouse are becoming one and this does not happen overnight.**

- Communication is the lifeblood of any marriage, so get real good at it.
- Keep the romance alive in your marriage.

Family

- Be aware of the communication filters that you have. Try to communicate with family members from a more accurate perspective of who they really are.
- Show honor and respect to your family, even when some of them don't deserve it.
- Improving familial relationships takes intentionality, prayer, guidance and persistence.

CHAPTER 5

Relationships (Dating, Friends, and Community)

Dating

D ating's evolution can be seen by glancing at history. In the late 1800s, dating (if you could even call it that) was primarily centered on functionality more than romance. People came together for their respective skills, such as childbearing, hunting, sowing, cooking and farming. Courtship became more romantic around the mid-1900s and couples coined the phrase "going steady" during this time. Dating was very likely to lead to marriage in this period. By the 1970s, society had loosened up quite a bit and people were more prone to date and have sex without any intention of forming an exclusive relationship. Dating services begin to pop up and game shows, such as "The Dating Game," became popular.

The disco and bar scene was vibrant during this time and there was less pressure to make a marital commitment before hitting the bedroom. The technological advances of the 1990s revolutionized the face of dating with people being able to communicate via email. Popular dating websites emerged, such as Match.com and eHarmony, making virtual dating possible. People are now able to create online profiles and get to know each other from the comfort of their own home. Speed dating and the club scene have now become very popular places to hook up with Mr. / Mrs. Right or Mr. /Mrs. Right Now.

It is important to understand dating as it pertains to relationships because there is a lot of inaccurate information circulating around. Dating can be a very beautiful and enjoyable thing if it is done for the right reasons. If not, it can be a source of great heartache and disappointment. Those who want to live an accurate life do not treat dating haphazardly. It is serious business.

The Purpose of Dating

Dating, when single, is meant to test the waters of compatibility with someone you are considering spending the rest of your life with. The dating process gives you a good idea of whether or not a "till death do us part" is feasible. Popular culture suggests that dating is for the express purpose of meeting people and having fun. While that is part of it, it is not the true purpose of dating.

Accurate dating means meeting someone with the intention of finding the person you will spend the rest of your life with. However, don't burden yourself with trying to make every person you date your husband or wife. I made that mistake early on. There should be an expectation that dating will lead to finding the person you will eventually marry, but that does not mean that you should have your mind fixed on marrying whoever you date. Dating is a means to an end when you are single.

With a firm foundation in place for why you are dating, you will not treat it as casually. Dating is not for the express purpose of having sex or even companionship (when you feel lonely). Popular media has a deceptive way of cheapening the true purpose of dating. Dating is seen as license to have multiple sex partners or several "friends" to choose from, depending on your need at the time. For example, I've heard people say that they date a certain person when they want to talk because that person is a good listener. They date another when they want to go out because that particular person has money and is able to pick up the bill. This type of dating is manipulative.

Be sure to keep the accurate idea of dating in mind as you engage in it, because it is easy to get carried away by popular opinions on the subject.

You Are Not Married Yet

I always tell single people to keep it light when dating someone. Even though your purpose for dating is to eventually find your future spouse, you don't want to make them your husband or wife after your first outing. I've made that error before with previous girlfriends. I've bought gifts and other special things that should have been reserved for my wife. I assumed that these people would eventually become my spouse, so I put the cart before the horse way too soon on a few different occasions.

Remember that you are still a single person when you are dating, even when you are "going steady." You do not become one until "I do" is said by both parties in holy matrimony. You can easily fall into the trap of acting like married people when you are dating someone consistently. There has to be a clear understanding up front that you two are getting to know one another during this time. There should be no other expectations during this period unless you both mutually consent to move further in the commitment.

Even once both parties agree to a deeper commitment, you have to keep in the forefront of your mind that you two are not an official item. This is often easier said than done, but if the correct perspective is kept in front of you, it will make it a little easier to safeguard your emotions. Dating should be a fun time of discovery for you and the other person. During this time you are finding your similarities, differences, quirks, irritations, goals, and visions.

To keep things less complicated in the dating relationship, you should not have sex. Physical intimacy is a surefire way to intensify the relationship before it is able to handle that shift. Unspoken expectations come after sexual intercourse. You actually become united in soul after having sex without proper marital legitimacy to back it. Some of my greatest heartbreaks occurred in dating relationships where we had intercourse. It took the fun and friendship aspect out of it. The relationship became emotionally unstable for both parties. Neither of us (in any of the cases) was ready to commit to a marriage, yet we had joined together as if we already had.

Healthy Dating

It is wise to not begin dating seriously until you are actually mature enough to get married. There is nothing wrong with having friendships with the opposite sex that have somewhat of a romantic influence in them, but that should be considered very different than dating someone. For example, you may still be a freshman in college but you are interested in someone in your class and would like to hang out with them. You know that you are nowhere near being ready for marriage, but you still want to enjoy someone's company by perhaps going out to a movie or some other activity. That's perfectly fine and even healthy in my opinion. But you should not make it a date.

Dating should only be reserved for those who are embarking upon the threshold of marriage. Simply put, dating is for the mature. We set ourselves up for failure when we take a dating mindset into a relationship between two individuals that are not mature enough to handle the prospect of marriage. You may ask, what is the difference between dating and just hanging out with someone you're interested in? The difference is found in the intent. Remember, the goal of dating is to eventually find your future spouse, whereas hanging out is just that and nothing more. Things are a lot lighter when you are just befriending someone of possible future interest to you. As you two grow and mature as individuals, you may then decide to begin dating one another. What qualifies as maturity? It can be defined as emotional stability, financial responsibility, and the ability to selflessly give yourself to another person. These are foundational to having a healthy marriage.

Our current societal paradigm does not promote or teach this line of thinking. It is assumed that you should date someone no matter what stage of life you find yourself. This leaves a lot of people severely wounded. They then end up taking very unhealthy baggage into future relationships. Remember that the majority of people are not concerned with living an accurate life, so don't be surprised if the way that you do things looks a lot different than the way they do. There will be a constant temptation to do things the way everyone else does, but you have to stick to your guns. What's more important: short-term acceptance or a lifetime of peace?

One of the best ways to date someone and keep it healthy is in group settings. For one, you get to see how this person is in social settings and it also takes some of the pressure off having to engage each other as a couple. Group dating also provides accountability if you are with other people who are seeking to live accurately. You will be less prone to have sex or fall into harmful behaviors that come with the bliss of dating. One point that I should make is that this principle is not rigid. Even though I am providing some insight on how to make the experience more enjoyable, experiences will look different for each individual. What I am presenting are some principles that will help you govern this beautiful and exciting process. As with anything, there has to be room allowed for human imperfection and misjudgment. I'm not trying to sound like Capt. Spoc from "Star Trek," but we humans have a lot of limitations that place a high demand on patience for one another.

When dating, you should find out one another's views toward marriage, money, family and life. Talk about these things often if you feel that you are forming a strong connection. The more you discuss them in the beginning, the less surprises there will be if you do tie the knot. Also, frequent communication will uncover irreconcilable differences that are warning signs for incompatibility. The majority of your time should be spent getting to know one another through talking and observation. A lot of people think dating just means cuddling up and whispering sweet nothings in each other's ears. Wrong! You are a scientist doing research on your possible mate. One of the chief reasons why so many marriages fail is because there was not enough due diligence given during the dating phase. Again, I'm not trying to make dating seem cold and impersonal, but there are a few switches on our brain that we need to make sure stay on when spending time with a prospective spouse.

Keep your heart open but also keep your mind alert. Emotions tend to blur good judgment. There are chemicals released in the brain called dopamine and norepinephrine when you begin getting close to someone who you have chemistry with. We don't want to counter that good feeling, but we do want to balance it out by keeping our wits during this critical period. It is wise to keep a close friend or a mentor whose words you value around while dating someone. Use them as a sounding board and listen to their wisdom. You will not be able to make the best decisions when you are in the love zone of dating on your own. I thank God that I had some really knowledgeable friends and mentors around me when I was dating and once I met my wife. Though I suffered my fair share of hurt, I was protected from grave mistakes that could have left me emotionally scarred long after some of these dating relationships ended.

I should also add, don't get into the habit of dating multiple people. You will do yourself and the person you are dating a huge disservice if you're spread thin emotionally. It takes years to learn some of the most basic qualities of people and a lifetime to understand their truly intricate nature. You may be able to multitask on your job, but it isn't wise to try juggling different potential life partners. If you do decide to date multiple people (which I strongly advise against), don't have more than two at a time and have the decency to tell them up front. Give them the option to decide whether or not that is OK. However, my honest and heartfelt opinion is that it is better to date only one person at a time.

Friends

Friendships are crucial to our development and often have direct impact on how far we are able to go in life. If you want to live an accurate life, you cannot choose your friends randomly. Your closest friends can make or break you. It has been stated by many financial gurus and world-renowned success coaches that your income is the average of that of your five closest friends. That ought to make you want to choose your friends a little more carefully.

True friends are hard to come by. I really believe that the majority of people have either associates or conditional friendships at best. When you find a true friend, one who is loyal and truly wants what is best for you (sometimes to their own loss); you need to hold on tightly. Earlier in the family section, I mentioned that friendships should be growing. You want to "do life" with people who you are able to develop with. Even though your friends are their own people, you do want to have friends who share many of the same core values as you. If they are not heading in the same direction as you, the friendship will not last or you will be extremely stressed out trying to preserve it.

Choose Your Friends Wisely

In friendships, it is always better to choose quality over quantity. I remember back in high school, my buddies and I would pride ourselves in how many so called "friends" we had in comparison to one another. It's called being popular. What I have grown to learn as an adult is that there are only a handful of people you can really rely on throughout life's winding roads. The same people who I called friends in high school would be the same ones talking bad about me if I got some bad locker-room press. At times, my truest friends were the most unlikely ones, and those who I thought had my back bailed on me. Don't just give anyone the title of friend because that is a position that must be earned and maintained.

Friends are people who are reliable and who want what is best for you. People who you just hang out with should not be given the designation of friend because these are associates. Friendship goes a lot deeper than just hanging out together. Friendship is proven by weathering storms of difficulty and coming out better as a result. Ninety percent of the "friendships" that we find ourselves in could not withstand some of the most basic problems without falling apart.

> *Not every friend will be one who you are to build something tangible with, but there should be something that you are both working toward together, even if it's just making each other better people.*

Accuracy requires precision, and this could not be any truer than in the area of friendships. Thus, you must choose your friends with extreme care. You don't want to be overly suspicious or paranoid, but you do want to put forth your due diligence when selecting your inner circle. "Do not be misled: Bad company corrupts good character," 1 Corinthians 15:33 maintains. There is a powerful truth contained in this statement. You will always become like those that you closely associate with. Accuracy requires you to associate with friends who will make you better and who will not allow you to be complacent.

Demonstrate What Being a Good Friend Looks Like

If you desire good friendships, you first have to be a good friend. You cannot control the behavior of others, only your own. Sometimes you may find yourself around people who will eventually grow into great friends, but you first must lay your life down for a season and show them how it is done. We must watch out for the unfair double standards that we place on people whom we are in relationship with. It is human nature to do this, but accuracy produces the ability to see our own faults first and where we are missing the mark. Once we deal with these issues in ourselves, we can then see clearly in order to help others work on theirs.

We should never require of others what we are unwilling to do ourselves. There has to be an initiator in every relationship in order for it to progress. If you are living a life of accuracy, you must be willing to take the lead. That means rolling up your sleeves and doing the dirty work of being reliable, selfless, and a good listener. When you provide this type of example, it will put positive pressure on those around you to follow suit, if they are true friends.

Differentiate Seasonal Friends from Lifetime Friends

One of the greatest lessons I have learned is to differentiate between lifetime friends and seasonal ones. There are certain people who come into our lives for a specific reason for an extended period of time. They may be there to help us accomplish something or overcome a great hurdle that we could not otherwise navigate through on our own. We can sometimes become resentful with these types of people if we don't understand what type of relationship we have with them. These types of relationships are not meant to last forever, only until what needs to be produced in you (and perhaps the other person) is realized.

Then there are other people who are meant to walk with us during our entire life journey. I like to call these types of friends' soul mates. It's as if Heaven has paired you with these friends at a deeper level and it transcends whatever season you find yourself in. If you have these types of friends, cherish them. These are the friends who always manage to keep turning up in your life, despite geographic location and the different paths that life will take you on. There is a special magnetism between lifetime friends that continues to draw them together.

I am fortunate enough to have a couple of friends like this. We do well to recognize that even though we have lifetime friends, there may be seasons where they are not in our lives. That is just how things work out sometimes. There are ebbs and flows in everything including relationships.

A Relationship Not Worth Risking Is Not Worth Having

True friendships require both parties to be honest with one another. The requirement is heightened in friendships where accuracy is the pursuit. It is human nature to try and not rock the boat too much and live in relative ease. But sometimes, healthy conflict and disagreement is needed in order to bring out the best in a friendship. I sometimes find myself under subconscious pressure to not tell people who are close to me things that I feel will eventually harm them if they don't change course. It is easy to become a big chicken with those that you care about because you want them to continue to like you and have good feelings toward you. But accurate friendships create room for sharpening one another or to put it another way, making one another better.

It is not wise to be reckless when giving constructive criticism and feedback to friends, but just know that if you feel extremely uncomfortable giving unpleasant information, you may need to reevaluate if what you have is a legitimate friendship. It may just be a glorified association. An accurate relationship welcomes transparency and candidness, and if these are not permitted in the friendship, it probably isn't a relationship that will endure.

My best friendships are the ones that allow me to be brutally honest about my struggles and triumphs without fear of being judged, ridiculed or taken out of context. Additionally, these relationships allow me to point out the flaws in my friends when I pick up on something that may be detrimental to them if left unchecked. Giving constructive criticism is risky business these days, when there are so many people who choose to live by their own truth. Yet, people committed to an accurate life hold themselves and those around them to a high standard and will seize the opportunity to discuss risky topics when they arise.

What Are You Building Together?

I am a firm believer that the greatest friends make the best partners for building something of worth and importance. My closest friends are those who I'm building something with. You may be building a business or an organization, or raising awareness for a cause and a friend is someone who is in the trenches with you helping you realize this vision. Not every friend will be one who you are to build something tangible with, but there should be something that you are both working toward together, even if it's just making each other better people.

Accuracy is never aimless; therefore, your friendships should have specific purposes. If they don't, you are probably just wasting time together. That may be fine for those who don't have accuracy in mind, but it is not acceptable for those who do. There needs to be a major overhaul and reevaluation of the definition of friendship. The popular notion of friendship has become very one dimensional and overemphasizes camaraderie as the main component. While companionship plays a big role in friendship, it is not the only aspect of it. Friendship also includes supporting one another in each other's endeavors. This support is not merely saying "attaboy" and giving each other high fives. It means to roll up the sleeves and help one another reach the visions placed in both parties' hearts.

So before you call someone your friend, or the all-too-common "best friend," examine if whether or not you are building something together.

The Importance of Growing Together

If you are a nice and affable person, you will accumulate all sorts of friends and associates of varying social, economic and educational backgrounds. Yet, you want to really cling to people who you can grow with. Friends who are a little beyond you in accomplishment and stability should be viewed as mentors or those you would like to emulate. Those who are a little behind you in these areas are more like mentees. You want to find friends who are in just about the same position as you so that you are growing together. This isn't to say that you may not one day grow a little further as time progresses. You want to be able to have someone who you can share your journey with, who is viewing it from a similar place. However, it is good to have friends that are in different statuses and stages of life.

I should add that having someone growing with you is important because if there is no growth, you may become complacent. We sometimes deceive ourselves into believing that we are better than we truly are because the company we keep is worse off than us. If we hung around friends who are as productive as we are or more, we would have a better sense of our true condition. Their growth will put pressure on you to reach for a higher standard.

When I speak about growth, I am referring to the process of increasing one's stature mentally, physically, spiritually, economically, relationally and professionally. There may be friends who you're growing with in only a couple of these areas (not every friend will be focused on increasing their stature in every section). That's fine, as long as you have some commonality in the growth process. Yet, you will more than likely find those friends who are growing in the same areas as you will be the ones who you form the strongest bonds with.

Mentally

What are your friends' thoughts on education, reading, increasing expertise and overall mental sharpening? What are your own? You should talk about the course of action you're taking and the priorities you share. This will give you both an idea of whether or not you are moving in the same direction and how deep your bond can grow in this area.

Physically

What level of importance do your friends place on physical fitness, diet and physiological well-being? Do they value this as much as you do? While this may not be one of the most important concerns in determining who our friends are, it is still wise to consider.

Spiritually

Are you and your friends in sync spiritually? Do you have the same faith and level of intensity for pursuing God? The best friendships that I have are those where I know I can have in depth conversations about God and not feel weird for doing so. I should reiterate that accuracy is deeply connected to having a strong relationship with God. Friends who don't share this passion may not be on the road to accuracy if their relationship with God is not top priority.

Economically

Do your friends have a healthy work ethic and are they pursuing financial freedom? How do they manage their money? Again, these are important things to talk about with them so you can know what level of influence you should allow the friendship to have on you in this area.

Relationally

Are you able to be transparent with your friends, and how do you both handle conflict? Can you count on them to be there for you when you need them? Is the relationship one-sided and based on convenience?

Are you both trying to improve your communication skills in order to better relate to one another?

Position

Would you consider you and your friends to be at a peer-to-peer level? Are you both pursuing similar positions and/or stations in life (does not have to be the same occupation)? Do the levels that you occupy in your current spheres of influence match, and/or will they eventually match should things work out according to the individual plans that you both have? If you and your friends have a similar position or capacity for a similar position, it will make it a whole lot easier to speak to one another from the same vantage point. For example, a general would understand another general's point of view quicker and more holistically than a sergeant would.

Community

The relationship that one has with his or her community is often a key indicator of what impact and legacy he or she will leave behind. Community is a loaded term, but in this book it can be defined as the groups of people with whom you find yourself interacting; they aren't family or people who work for the same employer as you do (business owners and entrepreneurs included). Your community can include your church, organizations you belong to, school, the city you live in, your social media outlets or wherever you interact with a group of people who have a common interest.

A person who lives an accurate life will always ask and reevaluate the reason why they are a part of the community that they belong to. They seek to better their communities and are proactive about forging strong relationships within them. Those on the path of accuracy often rise to become role models and leaders in their communities with or without a title.

Ask Why Are You in This Community

As I mentioned earlier, those who live an accurate life will always ask themselves why they identify with the community they find themselves a part of. They do this because it enables them to remain focused on how they can continue to better the community and be a contributing member. Those who do not ask themselves this question are more times than not either taking up space in the community or part of the problem found within it.

Community does not solely exist for the benefit of its members; the members have a role to play in ensuring that the community prospers and is progressing toward its respective cause. Therefore, you should know what role you play in your community and it should eventually be recognized by others. Imagine how powerful any community could become if all of its members were to approach it with this mindset.

> *Community does not solely exist for the benefit of its members; the members have a role to play in ensuring that the community prospers and is progressing toward its respective cause.*

Reevaluate the Reasons Why You're a Part of the Community

Reexamining why you are a part of a certain community has to do with your personal reflections as things within it progress. Events, people, processes and paradigms are always changing. So it is wise for us to give thought to how our roles change, expand, or retract as transition occurs in our personal lives and within our communities. We risk becoming obsolete or greatly disappointed if we aren't conscious of the vicissitudes around us. Any healthy community is growing, and with growth comes new opportunities and the discarding of what is no longer relevant.

Reevaluation of your role within a community also allows you to reaffirm your commitment to it. Many people allow several months and years to go by without assessing their functions and responsibilities. We have a tendency to go into "maintenance mode" and allow the same old operations to take place without giving thought to what is presently needed. In order to remain accurate in your community, you must set time aside for what I like to call "vision sessions." The purpose of a vision session is to take a step away from the monotony and everyday responsibilities in order to give thought to your current and future course of direction. In these gatherings, you can give clear thought to the role you play in your community. Community leaders should create retreats for the members in order to direct vision and articulate it to their people.

Impact Your Community

In chapter one, I briefly spoke about impact, which is one of the benefits of living accurately. One of my favorite movies of all time is *Kingdom of Heaven*. In the film, the newly appointed baron of Ibelin wasn't in his new estate for more than a week before he began fixing it up by building wells and a sophisticated irrigation system. The king's sister, Sibylla, who was visiting Balian of Ibelin's (the new baron) estate was very impressed and said, "It appears as if you will build a new Jerusalem." Balian replies, "What man is a man who does not make the world better?" There were 100 families living on Balian's land and it was very good land to start with. His father Godfrey, who left him the land and title, was wealthy. But Balian saw a need and that was for running water. He didn't rest on his laurels and kick up his heels; he instantly started to send positive ripples through his community.

No matter what condition you find your community in, you should seek to better it. The community should be better off by having you as one of its members. One of the greatest ways to make an impact in your community is to find a need and begin to create a solution for it. Even if you don't have much formal power and authority, you can still use whatever resources you have to help steer the community in a positive direction.

Immediately begin to seek ways to impart your knowledge and put your expertise to work in the community. It may be a thankless job at first, but rest assured that you will make an impact. There are many professional running backs who would never have accomplished the amount of yards they did without having a skilled full back blocking for them. Sometimes the community gets the glory instead of the individual, which should be the case anyway, but any community worth its weight will always acknowledge the positive effects that accurate individuals had on it.

Leave a Good Wake

If the time comes for you to leave your community and transition into another, as much as it depends on you, exit on a positive note. Henry Cloud notes in his book, *Integrity*, "One of my favorite things to do is to sit on the aft deck of a boat going across the ocean and just watch the wake. It is a beautiful, ever-changing creation as the ship continues on its path. You can tell a lot about a ship as you look at its wake. If it is in a straight line, you get a feeling that the boat is steadily on course, and that the captain is not dozing at the wheel, or that the engine shaft is not somehow out of whack. But if it is wavering you begin to wonder. ... In other words, what the wake looks like can tell you a lot about the boat itself."

Cloud goes on to express that people have wakes that they leave behind as well. There are two primary areas that are highlighted in a wake: task and relationship. Cloud poses this question, "What did he accomplish and how did he deal with people?" Is the community better because you were there, and did people benefit from your presence? Do community leaders have to put out fires that you caused, and do people have to recover emotionally from damage that you inflicted? From day one, we should seek to leave a good trail behind us and do our best not to leave until that is secured.

Lead With or Without a Title

Robin Sharma, author of *The Leader Who Had No Title*, asserts, "In many ways leading without a title is about the democratization of leadership. Yes, positions are important for the smooth running of any organization, whether it's a business, community or family. Having said that, the new model of leadership is all about every single stakeholder showing leadership in the work they do."

Don't wait until you're given a title before you start to lead. Leadership is not just management of others; we demonstrate leadership in making a needed contribution in a skillful manner without having to be asked. This could be something as simple as starting to clean up after a gathering and doing a phenomenal job at it. It could be expressed by executing whatever assignment you are given above and beyond the expectations of the person who gave it to you. Doing these types of things day in and day out will qualify you to obtain a title and formal position in whatever community you're involved.

I once heard a very high-profile community leader say that he only gives titles and formal recognition to those people who have already demonstrated the qualities that the particular title requires. People have a greater tendency to become complacent when they are given titles.

A title should only be a symbolic expression of what you are already functioning as.

Accuracy is more concerned with getting the job done than recognition. Our satisfaction comes in the form of our communities making progression. We can be just as effective if not more, without a title.

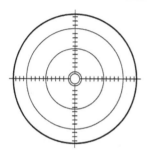

Scope of Accuracy – Aung San Suu Kyi

Aung San Suu Kyi has become an international symbol of freedom and human rights due to her staunch refusal to give in to the oppressive Burmese military led government. She recognized early on how corrupt the Burmese government had been for more than half a century and has made the establishment of democracy and justice in her country her life's work. In short, she is the Nelson Mandela of Burma. She spent more than two decades under house arrest by the Burmese government, which feared her as a political threat. The support of Suu Kyi's husband, Michael Aris, who lived in London, helped bring international exposure to Suu Kyi's political imprisonment.

However, Suu Kyi stayed under house arrest of her own volition. The Burmese government gave her a choice to either leave the country or stay under house arrest. Deeply committed to the cause of her community, people and country, Suu Kyi refused to leave. Her heroic decision led to international support from North and South America, Europe, Australia, India, Israel, Japan, the Philippines and South Korea.

During the 8888 Uprising, Suu Kyi was the voice that rallied the nation to oppose the current regime and find a way to bring reform to the Burmese government. Shortly after this, she was put under house arrest where she spent the next several years of her life. At great cost, she was not able to watch her sons grow up or be at the bedside of her husband who died from prostate cancer in 1999.

Suu Kyi has been the anchor of the Burmese people. Even without a formal title, she wielded great influence over her country and is regarded by many as the true leader of Burma. Mother Suu, as she is affectionately called, is still very much involved in the political reformation of her country and has plans to run for the Burmese presidency in 2015.

Honor Your Platform and the Bestower

Those who live an accurate life will generally be the ones who are chosen to move into positions of authority and influence in their respective communities. People just prefer to follow and trust those who demonstrate accuracy. With that said, we must learn the importance of treating the platforms given to us and those who bestow them on us with honor. It is especially hard to gain a true platform these days because everybody has access to one with the advent of social media and personal blogs. Everyone has a voice, so the idea behind a platform is greatly devalued. True places of influence should be treated with even greater respect because of their scarcity and just because it is overall good etiquette.

You show honor for your platform and those who grant it to you by publicly expressing your gratefulness to the community. These days, a platform can be a blog or it can be of the more traditional sort (e.g. a stage, pulpit, and lecture hall or conference room). Be thankful for those who lend you their platform and who allow you to influence their followers. Another way you honor your platform and the bestower is give your best performance when using it. Accuracy demands that you be well prepared, focused and ready to present your best work.

I constantly have to remind myself that it is a privilege to be on a platform within my community. When you have been on a platform for a while it is easy to forget this. But, there are many other people who would give their left arm to have the same opportunity. Sometimes we outgrow certain platforms and this is natural. But even when transitioning out and bringing someone else in, show honor to it and the one who gave you the opportunity. You never know when you may have to go back to that particular platform for an extended season or if you'll need the influence from it to help you progress. I've learned many of these lessons the hard way.

When I was just starting out professionally in music, a lot of major opportunities were presented to me without having to work very hard for them. I did work hard, but there was an unusual ease that I had in gaining notoriety for my artistry initially. Needless to say, I did not honor the different platforms that I had at that time or those who gave them to me, inadvertently burning a lot of bridges in the process. I ended up taking a hiatus from music for about two years after I got married and when I decided to come back, it was hard to regain old alliances and rebuild past relationships. Part of that was due to how the music industry works. Not too many people care about you when you haven't done anything in a while (two years is an eternity in rap music). But on my end, I was a little immature and didn't know the concept of honoring those who entrusted me with their platform and I got spoiled because I was always on someone's stage. No one is God's gift to earth. We have to remain humble and appreciative.

So now I advise people, if you are doing something that warrants someone else allowing you to influence people connected to their platform (no matter how small), show respect. It will help sustain a thriving relationship and allow you to utilize the platform again when the need arises.

Add to Your Community

Here's an important question. Do people want to belong to your community as a result of you being part of it? What we demonstrate should cause outsiders to want to be part of what we do. If we provide the right example of what our community is like, people will be drawn to it. The thought we want to run across the minds of the people we associate with should be, "If that's how they are because of the community they are in, I want to be a part of that community as well."

Another thing to keep at the forefront of our minds is that we are a representative of whatever community we belong to. With that said, we want to make our communities proud and bring honor to them with our actions and lifestyle. I love when I hear people say they want to check out things that I am a part of, especially if I am the only symbol associated with it that they have come across.

Adding to our respective communities also consists of bringing resources back that will benefit them. This could come in the form of some sort of specialized training you can use to help others. I was once part of a community that had a very financially astute member who held classes on investments for the other members free of charge. You may be someone who can connect visionaries in your community with outsiders who have the resources to make their dreams a reality. Or perhaps you have networked with grant writers or investors who believe in the vision and personnel within your community. Accurate people are always looking to add value to whatever they are members of.

Application of Accuracy

Dating

- **Remember that dating is about finding your future spouse — don't treat it flippantly.**
- **Try to keep the dating relationship as light as possible to avoid heartache in case it doesn't work out.**
- **Dating should only be reserved for those who are embarking on the threshold of marriage.**

Friends

- **Choose your friends wisely. We become like those with whom we closely associate.**
- **If you desire to have good friendships, you first have to demonstrate that you are a good friend.**
- **Find friends who you can grow and build something with.**

Community

- **Always seek to better whatever community that you are a part of.**
- **Continue to reevaluate why you are part of a particular community.**
- **Lead with or without a title.**
- **If you get a title, honor your platform and those who give it to you.**

Chapter 6

Relationships
(Associates and Enemies)

Associated

Associates, in this context, are those who are not friends, family or enemies. Rather, they are neutral people who you may come into contact with on a regular basis. These relationships often go overlooked because they aren't as intense as the other types, but they are important relationships to maintain and cultivate as well. The ever-increasing interconnectedness of our world places a greater responsibility on those pursuing accuracy to manage their associations well.

Everybody Knows Somebody

More than likely, you have heard of the concept of six degrees of separation. The notion behind this thought is that everyone is connected to someone who is connected to someone of great influence who can dramatically affect their life. Experience has taught me that life-changing events can be determined by a small conversation between a decision maker and one of his relatives (who happens to be one of the person's associates). It blew my mind when I found out how some people got promoted or demoted in organizations. It's not always a long, drawn-out process when it comes to choosing who gets access to greater resources and authority in a company or organization. It is very closely related to associations.

Sometimes opportunities are given just because someone says that they like you or, on the flipside, you could spend several years in a corporate dungeon because you were rude to the receptionist, who just happens to have the ear of the CEO. From this knowledge, I now seek to treat all of my associates with respect and do whatever is in my power to leave a good taste in their mouth when my name is brought up. You can't please everyone, but you can do your best to make as few enemies as possible.

If you are living an accurate life, you will draw some attention. Remember, there is always somebody watching you. Their word alone may be enough to help you progress or stay trapped in a position that you don't care for. I don't want to give people too much credit though because God ultimately determines how high someone elevates in any company, organization or community.

Do What Is Right in the Eyes of Outsiders

The Apostle Paul instructs his protégé Timothy in his book 1 Timothy, that leaders in his church "must have a good reputation with outsiders so that he will not fall into disgrace and into the devil's trap" (1 Timothy 3:7, NIV). This is a universal principle that doesn't relate solely to communities of faith. A life of integrity and moral character carries tremendous weight and has a profound effect, not only within our inner circles but on our associates as well. You may not hear many people voice their respect and admiration for you if you are doing things right, but you'll never hear the end of it if you drop the ball, especially in matters of integrity and morality.

One of the greatest shockers of our time is when employers began to go on social media websites and look up their employees or potential candidates. There have been many people who have lost jobs and other opportunities based on what a Google search showed. There are more eyes on us than ever before, which means we have to really be who we want others to believe that we are. Accurate people carry themselves well when in all places, be it the barber shop or hair salon, restaurants or the movies.

We all have make mistakes. None of us should necessarily try to walk on the tightrope of human approval. That is exhausting, but our natural conduct should be what people deem admirable and worthy of respect. We should live lives that reflect the amount of people and the grade of people we want at our funerals. I want my funeral to be packed and have among the diverse attendees' high-profile and highly respected people.

What about you? If you were to die today, what type of home going ceremony would you have?

Turn Associates into Close Acquaintances

Right around the time I was getting ready to release my third album, *Anno Rebelio*, there was a young lady by the name of Ashley who I would bump into often at my church. Finally one day I decided to strike up a small conversation with her. It turned out that Ashley was an entertainment journalist and had skills that I needed to promote my new effort. As we spoke, we both had common interests in entertainment and ended up developing a professional respect for one another. She ended up creating some promotional materials and giving me some marketing ideas that were very useful for the success of my project. Ashley Ratcliff is also the one who edited this book that you are now reading. How cool is that?

You'd be amazed at what striking up a light conversation can lead to. There is so much wealth in people that we walk past on a day-to-day basis that it would take our breath away once we uncovered it. It's not about getting something out of people; it's about seeing the value of their experiences, perspectives and talents. One of the reasons I am writing this book is because of a conversation that I had with a co-worker who planted a seed in me to become an author. If we hadn't had that encouraging dialogue, who knows if I would be pursuing this dream now?

We should seek to deepen our bonds with associates who we come into contact with on a regular basis. It would be very disappointing if you found out that your process in a particular area of life could have been greatly accelerated had you sat down and had a meaningful conversation with an associate. With that said, good judgment must be used. Not everyone who is an associate deserves a closer relationship with you and vice versa. Yet, everyone who we come across regularly should not just be taken at face value. Everybody has a story that is worth hearing.

Enemies

Alas, we get to the juicy topic of how accurate minds interact with enemies. There are many different viewpoints and directions that I could apply to this matter, but the best one I've seen is from the teachings and life of Jesus Christ. The way that we interact with our supposed enemies has a profound impact on our overall wellbeing and progression. Let's hear what the dynamic rabbi has to say about the topic of enemies.

> "But I tell you who hear me: Love your enemies, do good to those who hate you, bless those who curse you, pray for those who mistreat you. ... If you love those who love you, what credit is that to you? Even sinners love those who love them. And if you do good to those who are good to you, what credit is that to you? Even sinners do that." (Luke 6:27-28, 32-33, NIV)

This is a revolutionary view on how to relate to ones enemies. Accuracy would have us respond in a positive manner to those who treat us wrongly. That concept goes totally against what the majority of us have been taught. There is a natural tendency in people to get even and seek retribution for their losses. However, we are instructed by the most accurate person who ever walked this planet to follow a much higher standard, His standard.

Operate in Integrity

We all have mishaps and make mistakes. None of us should necessarily try to walk on the tightrope of human approval. That is exhausting, but our natural conduct should be what people deem admirable and worthy of respect.

If you know someone is out to get you or for whatever reason is in strong opposition toward you, one of the best defenses is to live an honest life. That means, what you see is what you get. You demonstrate that what you say is what you mean and your actions back the words that come out of your mouth. To take it further, you not only want to be honest, but you want exemplary conduct to be a habit for you. This will take the fuel out of any allegations or grudges your enemies may have against you.

It is hard to rationally oppose someone who is living in an upright matter. Notice, I said rationally though. There will always be those special individuals who choose to provoke you just because and they can deceive themselves into thinking they have just cause for doing so. The good thing about walking in integrity is that these silly people will be exposed to others and the truth will be clearly seen by those who have good sense. You shouldn't worry about appeasing those who choose to believe lies.

Pray for Them

Earlier in the book, I discussed that prayer is one of the main ways that we relate to God. The other great facet of prayer is that it can be a great offensive weapon in terms of diffusing tensions between you and your enemies. If you earnestly pray that God would move on your enemies hearts and cause their feelings toward you to change, He will. At the very least, He will cause you to have tremendous peace when dealing with them so that their actions don't affect you to the degree that they could.

Whenever I told my grandfather that I was having an issue with someone, he would respond every time in his country drawl, "Just pray fer 'em." That was his answer to everything. I think a man who makes it well into his 90's deserves to be listened to. We don't place high enough importance on prayer and intercession, which is prayer on behalf of others, in today's culture. I think many have bought into the notion that prayer doesn't work or it isn't practical.

Prayer should be as normal as breathing or talking on a cell phone. In essence, that's what it is. Put some genuine heartfelt prayer on your enemies for at least 30 days and I guarantee you will notice some sort of change in them, in you or in the environment in which you both occupy. Our human nature can get the best of us when we are in a conflict with someone, and in order for us not to make a messy situation worse we need someone with greater wisdom and insight to intervene. Who better than God Himself?

My grandfather would tell me that there's no whooping worse than a whooping that is given by God. I should reiterate that our goal is not to see our enemies get a whooping (unless they really deserve it), but God will bring trouble on those who trouble people striving to live a life that pleases Him. So as you pray that God blesses your enemies and changes their heart, God may very well take the liberty to change their heart but pull out his invisible belt as well. He loves your enemies too, so there is a good chance that they need it. I must add, don't gloat over your enemies if something negative does come their way. That is the quickest way to lose your favor with God.

Seek to Get an Understanding

Oftentimes, people become our enemies for some of the silliest reasons. We may have forgotten to acknowledge them on a particular day or we didn't return a phone call. Different personalities take offense to different things. There are offenses that one person can brush off that another person loses sleep over and causes them to hold a grudge for the next 30 years. That's just life.

> *Our enemies, or those we have conflict with, often expose the chinks in our armor that we ourselves and those who like us overlook.*

You and I can't control that. But what we can do is seek to get an understanding of the wrong (real or perceived) someone feels that we caused them.

You'd be surprised what a 20-minute conversation over a cup of coffee could clear up. What I am learning is that the human imagination has a way of magnifying the smallest things. It is no different in conflict. Once we begin to believe something about someone, every action that they take that fits our description of them becomes what we store away in our memory files. In reality, they could be as self-sacrificing as Mother Teresa, but one trespass could cause us to only see how they put too much mustard on their hot dog and that they only gave $1 to the homeless guy instead of $20. It sounds silly, but that is what we all do sometimes.

Communication can dispel all of this or confirm how much of a jerk you were to them so you can apologize. We should do whatever is in our power to improve a negative relationship. I have found that what people want most often is just to be understood. They want to know that you care about them. Sometimes people will take offense because you want to be accurate. It inadvertently puts pressure on them to do the same and they could grow to despise you because of that. Therefore, we must humble ourselves and show genuine acceptance of those who may not be ready to turn that leaf in their life. You won't be able to please everyone, but at least they will know that you're a human and not just an accuracy-chasing robot. Plus, living a life of accuracy is a calling that people have to choose to embrace.

Help people come to their own terms on why they consider you an enemy. Sitting down and talking with them will force them to give specific occurrences that have caused an issue. If they can't come up with a specific reason, then hopefully they will see that their dislike for you stems from their own personal issues. But if they do list specific reasons for their disdain, then you have something that you can both work toward to rectify. We have to be willing to listen to them and make adjustments in our actions if they point out areas where we're dropping the ball. This is a pivotal aspect of living accurately. Our enemies, or those we have conflict with, often expose the chinks in our armor that we ourselves and those who like us overlook.

Be Respectful

Just because someone is our so-called enemy doesn't mean that we should be disrespectful to them. Sure, there are moments that we all have where we would like to vent our frustration toward those who aren't favorably disposed toward us. We have to keep our head though and remember that our opponents are people, too, with their own struggles. We shouldn't give them more reason not to like us.

In *The Art of War*, Sun Tzu speaks of having a healthy respect for one's enemies. Even warring opponents can show honor to one another. Sometimes I have to watch the words that come out of my mouth when I am speaking about those who I'm not too fond of. Words carry tremendous creative power and they send out an energy that can either create or absolve relational tension. People are able to pick up on when someone has been talking negatively about them.

We will sometimes have enemies who are not worthy of respect because of the way they carry themselves. We should show respect nonetheless. Demonstrating respect has more to do with you and your character than it does with appeasing them. If we carry ourselves in a respectable manner and show deference to others (including enemies), it further solidifies our character and reputation. There is something powerful demonstrated in a person who doesn't succumb to a lower level when other people employ those methods toward them.

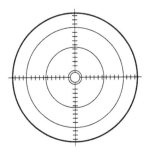

Scope of Accuracy- Sun Tzu

Arguably, the most revered military mind of all time is Sun Tzu; author of the military classic The Art of War. *There are many disagreements about Sun Tzu's origins and history. However, most scholars agree that he served as general and strategist to King Helü of Wu China during the late sixth century. Sun Tzu's strategies, tactics and teachings have lived long beyond his time. Today,* The Art of War *is listed on the Marine Corps Commandant's Professional Reading program. During the Gulf War, generals Colin Powell and Norman Schwarzkopf Jr. utilized the Sun Tzu principles of speed, attacking the enemy's weak points and deception. The Vietnamese general who routed American and French forces during the Vietnam War was a pupil and user of Sun Tzu's teachings.*

Some of Sun Tzu's most popular principles are:

- *To win 100 battles is not the height of skill, to subdue the enemy without fighting is.*
- *Know your enemy and know yourself and 100 battles you will never be in peril.*
- *Attack the enemy's weakness, not his strength.*
- *It is more important to outthink your opponent than to outfight him.*

Do Not Become Bitter

Bitterness is something that we must be careful to guard against. It is a sneaky vice and must be checked daily. It can be revealed in an overly cynical and pessimistic attitude. Sometimes it lies dormant under the surface without our awareness and then exposes itself during stressful times. Bitterness is a soul killer that will leave you destitute. I have seen many promising people become its prey and struggle to recover from its grip. You never want to give any person that kind of power over your life. You can protect yourself from bitterness in a number of ways.

Encourage Yourself Daily: Train your mind to look for the good in life. Being around people who have negative feelings toward us can suck the joy out of life. Remembering your positive qualities, contributions and potential future can help you blast out bitterness when it tries to set in. We have to vigorously set our minds on what encourages us. According to *Psychology Today*, more than 70 percent of the average person's thoughts are negative.

Stay Connected to God: Keep a strong bond with God and let Him soothe your soul. Shed your tears and heartache in His presence when you are alone and let Him heal your mind with His word (the Bible). Develop endurance for fellowshipping with God and take time to reflect on His goodness toward you. A great book on this is *The Practice of the Presence of God* by Brother Lawrence.

Keep Proper Perspective: There is always a reason behind what you are going through that serves a greater purpose in your overall development. Search out what that reason may be, write it down and reflect on it often. This will guard your heart from self-pity, which is a very destructive emotion. Proper perspective elevates your viewpoint and enables you to see the good in any hardship.

Find Someone Trustworthy to Talk With: Having an outlet to express your emotions is a tremendous defense against bitterness. Talking out how you feel can be very therapeutic and help alleviate some of the frustration. Plus, a trustworthy confidant can also provide a more accurate perspective and encourage you through your ordeal. Women are usually better at this than men, but this is a very useful tactic for both genders to employ.

Don't Lose Your Cool

A well-respected leader once told me a story involving him and another high-ranking leader in the city. The leader, we'll call him Allen, was putting on a huge citywide event that would attract thousands of people. Allen and this particular leader, who we'll call Tom, were very close, but this event created somewhat of a tension between them. Instead of supporting Allen, Tom spoke badly about this event and wouldn't allow those whom he had influence over to really get behind it. What's worse, when one of Tom's followers brought him a stack of promotional material for the event, Tom threw them in the trash.

This truly broke Allen's heart because he thought they were friends. Allen was not trying to outdo Tom; he simply had a vision that was very big and thought it would be good for the city. For a long time, Allen was very hurt by Tom's actions but he didn't retaliate. He knew it would have brought upheaval to the city should these two key leaders engage in conflict. So he held himself together. Sometime later, Tom came to his senses and realized how selfish he had been and now Tom is one of Allen's greatest supporters for his citywide vision. Allen turned what could have been a lifetime enemy into a friend and even greater alliance.

What I learned from this story is that your greatest opponent can become your greatest cheerleader if you respond accurately. It clearly would have been in Tom's best interest had Allen chose to fight fire with fire. Allen's event and reputation could have been discredited if he gave in to his emotions. Choosing to refrain from anger is one of the hardest things to do, especially when it is justified. We all can probably attest. But operating from a place of anger always does more harm than good.

There have been words spoken in moments of anger that the receiving party will never be able to forget and truly move past. A wound inflicted by a sharp tongue is hard to heal. It is better to take a walk and go yell at the ocean than at another person. We just don't bounce back that easily. There are certain instances where you and I may have to address our enemies verbally, but even then it should be done with a level head. We need to be able to articulate their error, get an understanding of why they did it and how to resolve the issue at hand even if they are raving like a lunatic.

Your Advancement Is Beyond the Control of Your Enemies

I once had a supervisor who I was sure hated my guts. More than anything, I think she was a little intimidated that I had a good relationship with the CEO of the company. I was a hard worker and showed the capacity to be a supervisor as well. There was a special training for a new project at work that I was slotted for. Upper management was positioning me to become a supervisor for this particular assignment.

I was still currently under the supervision of this person who didn't like me though. This person tried everything in her power to prove that I was incompetent and incapable of being a supervisor. The supervisor made sure to point out any errors that I made on paperwork and anything else that could have disqualified me for the new position. She honestly did a good job; I thought my promotion was as good as gone. I was angry at this person; I couldn't understand why she would want to sabotage my advancement.

Psalm 37 became my best friend during this season of life. I was reminded that I should entrust myself to God, who is the only being that has the power to promote, and continue to do good. That meant not trying to fight against this supervisor, but concentrate on continuing to do great work. About six months later I got that promotion and less than a year later I got another promotion. I learned a very powerful principle of accuracy from this. Advancement is beyond the control of your enemies. If there is a position for you to occupy, there is no one but you who can keep you from getting there.

Often, before you obtain a promotion there is a time of testing. The time of testing is used to refine you and strengthen your character before you get the new position. The Navy Seals go through 30 months of brutal training before they are allowed to become a part of the military's elite. The rationale behind this is that training like lives are at stake equips them to handle the moments when lives are truly at stake.

Many people give up if they catch enough opposition from people. Sometimes we fail to recognize that these very people are being used to sharpen and make us more accurate for our greater assignment. We easily forget our training when it takes place in the real world. There can be difficulty in recognizing that training is taking place when you have a sales team that doesn't follow orders or students who don't respond to your teaching. Rest assured, you are being molded in these moments of adversity and your enemies are just the tools that God is choosing to use. You will make it to your destination if you hang in there.

Don't Lose Who You Are

Sometimes when we deal with back-to-back conflicts, we tend to go into our metaphoric shells or even put on a mask to protect ourselves from the outside world. This has a lot to do with our survival instincts and it is one of the most basic features of being human. Yet, you and I never want to go so far into a shell that we don't know how to come back out. There are many people who once had a pure heart toward their vision and other people, but the wounds inflicted by their enemies turned them into master manipulators and hustlers. They now thrive on making other people prey and misuse them to get to their destination. They still have a clear and compelling vision for their life, but the means they use to obtain it is destructive.

I know other people who go to the opposite extreme; they just become a pacifist and don't ever rock the boat, even if their vision would demand it. They cowardly turn inward and won't risk being disliked so they can maintain whatever security they think they have. What's worse, these types begin to criticize others who have the guts to go after their God-given potential and passive aggressively try to block them. There is a great temptation for you and I to become like this because most people don't like conflict. I certainly don't. My palms get sweaty and I get super nervous if I know I am going into an environment that is against me.

We have to learn how to play well despite adversity. This is a very hard discipline to learn. Our very make-up is tested when we are engaged in the fires of conflict. If you are a good-natured and well-meaning person, these tests will either strengthen your capacity for goodness for or make it deteriorate. If you are a person of integrity, a barrage of enemies will reveal how strong your resolve is concerning that character trait — and this is a good thing!

Oswald Chambers brilliantly stated, "Faith must be tested, because it can only become your intimate possession through conflict." I will put my own twist on those words and say that true virtue can become our intimate possession only through conflict. A popular truism accurately asserts, "If you falter in times of trouble, how small is your strength" (Proverbs 24:10). Being challenged by others who don't like us is a wonderful opportunity to express our true character, not disregard it.

I saw a great scene in *Machine Gun Preacher,* a film about an ex-biker turned preacher who helps protect children in Africa from the Lord's Resistance Army (LRA) which is abducting them and turning them into children soldiers or sex slaves. From the title, you can see that this minster employs unusual methods for a person of the cloth, using heavy artillary and other weapons to rescue children and bring them back to the church he has built. During the battle with the LRA, Sam Childers, portrayed by

Gerard Butler, begins to lose his grasp on reality and begins to develop hatred in his heart. He starts to become obsessed with war and loses perspective on why he is trying to help the kids. The pastor becomes a little scary to be around and his family and those who follow his leadership feel he can't be reached anymore. In a touching scene, one of the kids that Childers has rescued comes and sits next to him on his bedside (a child that he didn't know could speak English) and says to the distraught minister, "We can't let them steal our hearts. When they take our hearts, they have won."

The words of this child in this movie really resonated with me. As you and I pursue a life of accuracy, we cannot let our hearts — the core essence of who we are — be stolen by people, forces or circumstances that oppose us. Our accomplishments and external demonstrations of accuracy will mean nothing if we lose the love within our hearts. As we move into the next chapter of this book, I hope that you will reflect on and revisit this one from time to time. Relationships are and will always be the greatest currency in any society.

> *Advancement is beyond the control of your enemies. If there is a position for you to occupy, there is no one but you who can keep you from getting there.*

Application of Accuracy

Associates

- Remember that everybody knows somebody. Treat everyone well.
- Carry yourself in such a way that earns the respect of outsiders.
- Strike up conversations with people who you see fairly regularly. You never know where it could lead.

Enemies

- Live an honest and upright life. Be who you say you are. This will take the fuel out of any allegations an enemy may try to bring against you.

- Pray for your enemies. There is nothing more effective than prayer when it comes to fixing a negative relationship.
- Seek to get an understanding of your enemy and why they may be upset with you.
- Show respect always and keep your cool when dealing with enemies.

SECTION III

FINANCES, OCCUPATION, BUSINESS AND ENTREPRENEURSHIP

We cannot ignore the fact that how we manage our finances is a key indicator of how well we manage our lives. Those who are able to gain control of their financial resources often end up with more peace of mind and time to do what they really care about. One's occupation is a vehicle that allows us to learn and express accuracy in a variety of ways while earning income in the process. Some people are able to cross the threshold of having a job to creating jobs. Those who become proficient in the areas of business and entrepreneurship stand as symbols of accuracy of the highest caliber because they have learned how to create something out of nothing and make it sustainable for the benefit of others.

CHAPTER 7

Finances

The subject of finances is massive and would take another book for me to expound upon. So what I'll do is give some brief and simple principles that I have either observed and/or employed that have brought about accuracy. I will also list resources, books and give mention of financial rock stars that knock it out of the park consistently. I want to remind you that the goal of this book is to make you hungrier to chisel away at the mountain of accuracy with your own personal due diligence and research. Let this be somewhat of a guide and igniter to stimulate wholesome thought and motivate action.

Determine Your Value System

The common mindset of today is to get more. Since we live in a more affluent society (in North America at least), there is the pressure to spend our hard-earned money on things to impress people we don't even really like. The people who truly like us shouldn't be deterred in their relationships with us if we don't keep up with the Joneses. It is not up to me to determine your value system; rather, you must develop it on your own based on what your purpose is. The important thing is to determine your value system and let that help guide your financial decisions. David Bach, author of *Smart Couples Finish Rich*, gives a great definition of what a value is in the form of a question. Bach asks, "What is it that you stand for and what is it that you care most deeply about? In other words, what are your values?" Before we dive into this section of finances, I want you to give some thought about what comprises your value system. Do your values place the most importance on luxury, security, financial freedom, being able to give or being able to travel? These are just some examples of what constitute values. Now hold on to that thought as we move forward.

Budgeting

I have to be honest with you. I didn't know a lick about budgeting until I met my wife. The best I knew to do was write down what I thought I was going to earn in a month and what my expected expenses were. I wrote these down on a yellow note pad and tried to keep track with this sloppy system from month to month. Thank God for my wife! She introduced me to a more sophisticated and less complicated way of budgeting finances, which we still use to this day.

Sometimes budgeting gets a bad rap and many people prefer not to deal with their financial woes because they are scared of what they may find. I was the same way. I had debt and I was broke. My little dysfunctional budgeting system helped me keep up the illusion that everything was OK. But it was just a fallacy. The moment I employed true budgeting in my life, I gained a power and freedom that I never had before. It is better to know what your problems are than to be in the dark. You have no hope of finding a solution if you remain oblivious to your financial condition.

There are many tools to use in order to budget. My wife and I use Excel spreadsheets, which are set up for a bi-weekly pay period since that is typically how our income is paid to us. We have different sections in the spreadsheet for our different income types and expenses. We have a separate budget spreadsheet for our businesses. Under the income section, we have subheadings in which we enter all our different types of income (e.g. wages, dividends, etc.). Under the expenses section, we have the subheadings of home, tithes/offering, daily living, transportation, entertainment, health, personal, debt and miscellaneous. We have another section that reflects all of our different savings, such as our retirement, emergency, house, vacation and any other things we may need money for in the future.

Through our budget, we know where every single penny is allocated, what bills need to be paid, and have a record of our financial activity from year to year in order to compare our progress. When we first started doing our budget together, it was a little rocky. We both had our ideas of where the money should go, but since then we have matured and are able to work more as a team. The hardest part of a budget is sticking to it. But if you do, you will be better off financially and have peace at night, at least the peace of knowing how deep your financial hole is.

Budgeting is an easy step to take in financial accuracy. It just takes a willingness to create one and stick to it. Much of the budgeting software out today already has templates that make it even easier to set up. Go over your budget regularly, once a week at least. My wife and I have found that reviewing our budget brings us closer together, and cuts down on arguments and miscommunication because we are both on the same page. Don't be intimidated by budgeting. It is a simple yet critical element to living an accurate life. The most financially successful people and families are those who talk about money often. Just like anything, the more that you budget the better you will become at it and it will not take as much effort.

Saving

I am a saver by nature. While my wife is the budgeting guru, I am definitely the reigning champ when it comes to saving. I think part of the reason I am like this is because I have seen a lot of people who were at one time financially well off fall on hard times and have nothing to show for their hard work. I determined as a young child to never let that happen to me (at least if I could help it).

I had to learn the hard way that saving should not be done in a hoarding type of fashion. It is one thing to go without certain luxuries, but you should never subject those around you to a poor quality of life just so you can save a few extra dollars (unless, of course, they are in agreement). Saving should be fun and there should be a goal in mind when doing it. Saving money just to save it is foolish. Money should always serve a purpose greater than just being able to say that you have a ton of money in the bank. That is what I like to call the Scrooge syndrome.

Oh, you've heard of Scrooge haven't you (if not, check out the movie *A Christmas Carol*)? When my wife and I first got married, we moved back to California where my first "real" job out of college was. As a new husband, I feared for our financial future and sought to save every single dime I could find. I went without haircuts some weeks and frowned upon my wife buying extra items of clothing here and there, as was her custom before we were married. I was a Scrooge in the making and didn't know it. We amassed a nice little nest egg, but we were both miserable because of my miser-like tendencies.

I don't know when it happened, but I finally got the memo and loosened up on our cash flow so we could begin to enjoy life a little. Now I am a lot more balanced when it comes to saving because my viewpoint is a little more mature. So if you are a newlywed reading this book, hang in there! Your spouse will eventually turn around with enough prayer. There are four different types of savings funds that you may want to consider having. You may come up with more or less, but it is my experience that these are the most fundamental savings: retirement, emergency, investment and the WWW (what I've termed "What We Want" savings).

Retirement

Dave Ramsey talks about retirement in his amazing book, *The Total Money Makeover*. He asserts, "When I speak of retirement, I think of security. Security means choices. (That's why I think retirement means that work is an option.) You can choose to write a book, to design churches, or to spend time with your grandkids. You need to reach a point where your money works harder than you do." That is how I like to think of retirement. I still plan to work after I am retired; the only thing is I will be choosing to work rather than obligated. I will be able to freely work on my passions without having to be tied down by a paycheck.

One of the most disheartening things that I witness are those elders well into their seventies who are working at the checkout stands of Target and greeting people at the doors of Walmart. Many are there not because they want to be, but because they have to be. For whatever reason, their financial life didn't keep up with their physical life and they are forced to do a job that is probably well below their wisdom and expertise. I'm not trying to malign them; honest work is honest work. But I'm sure if you asked many of them what they would rather being doing with the latter years of their life; it isn't pushing baskets across a parking lot. Therefore, it is imperative for those of us in pursuit of an accurate life to learn from them and cause our situation to be different.

There are a lot of schools of thought as it relates to retirement planning. I won't really get into all of that. You determine the best way to get to your goals. What I want to drive home is that you begin to give serious thought to what your retirement plan is going to be while you are still young (or have a good amount of working years ahead of you). I recommend that you read books on retirement planning and even higher a trusted consultant to help you put together a workable game plan.

Start with saving a portion of all income that you make (I recommend at least 10 percent) and put that into a separate retirement account such as a 401(k) or Roth IRA (individual retirement account). It is a lot easier to save this money if you have it automatically deducted from your paycheck. Many employers will match your savings contribution by up to five percent. If you work somewhere that has a 401(k) retirement savings match, take full advantage of it. Be sure that you become very knowledgeable about whatever investment vehicle(s) you use for your retirement.

The Emergency Fund

Living paycheck to paycheck, unfortunately, is the condition that the majority of people find themselves in. That means that if they were to lose their job or if some catastrophic event happened, it would rock their financial world and they may end up out of house and home. An emergency fund is a safeguard against the rainy seasons of our lives. Less-than-optimal times are sure to come. They come in the form of unexpected car repairs, emergency room visits, frozen bank accounts and company downsizings, among other blows. An emergency fund is a hedge of protection against these problems.

Most finance experts agree that it is wise to save up to three to six months of money needed to cover expenses. Some even go as far to say 12 months, depending on what type of occupation you have. For example, if you are an employee of the government and have been at your job for 15-plus years and there have been no signs of instability, three to six months of an emergency fund should do the trick. However, we have seen as of late that not even the government is untouchable. If you are a salesperson who lives off of commissions and each month can either be feast or famine, then it is wise to set aside 12 months or more for covering expenses.

The goal of saving three months to a year's worth of expenses can be a little daunting at first. But fret not — start with saving $1,000 first. Dave Ramsey advises that you do whatever it takes to get to that $1,000, even if you have to sell some items. This first $1,000 is a critical threshold to cross. For one, saving this initial amount will give you a quick victory, which is necessary for gaining greater momentum. For more on emergency funds, I suggest reading Ramsey's *The Total Money Makeover*.

Investment

The investment savings is something of my own devising. I'm sure there is someone smarter than me who came up with it first, but I have a little twist on this type of savings account. The investment savings is for the purpose of having seed money to parlay into money-making vehicles. Your typical investment savings account would be for stocks, bonds, real estate, treasury bills, mutual funds and money market accounts.

My little twist is this: I believe that part of your investment savings account should be used to invest in you. I once heard someone say that you are your greatest investment. There is no other investment that will produce a better ROI (return on investment) than you. Plus, an investment in you cannot be lost. Sure, you may make a few mistakes, but this is just the tuition you pay in the School of Accuracy.

Therefore, it is this author's recommendation that you set aside money for a business, product, service, invention, advanced degree, certification, credential or a piece of equipment that will allow you to create wealth on your own terms. This will give you great satisfaction and increase your value as a person. A man or a woman who invests in his or herself has less chance of going hungry than someone who depends on a handout from someone who has invested in themselves. The important thing is to do something that you are passionate about.

Investing

Let me ask you a question. Let's pretend that you are the owner of a construction company and you have landed a contract to build 100 homes for a city. Would it be more prudent to build all of these homes yourself (just you) or hire a crew of other professionals to build the homes while you carefully oversee this massive project? Anybody in their right mind would choose the latter of the two options. We can both agree that it would be a lot better and quicker to have a team under you building these homes whether you are at the job site or not.

Investing is pretty much the same principle. You work hard for your money; the trick is to learn how to get your money to work harder than you whether you lift a finger or not. Investing allows you to leverage the assets of another entity in order to share in the profits (or losses). The favorite investment vehicles of the world's most successful investors historically has been the stock market, real estate and promising startup companies with a great product.

This type of investing is different from the type that I mentioned a little earlier; they involve investing your money in outside opportunities. A balanced investment strategy would be to invest some of your capital in a wealth-generating venture that you create and one (or a few) that is outside of your control that you really believe in. One outside entity that I am really excited about is real estate. I spend a lot of time reading books and learning about real estate investing so that I am prepared to go into this sector with a running start. Widely heralded investor Warren Buffett said that he doesn't invest in something unless he understands it. He said that Facebook is a great company, but he wouldn't invest in it because he doesn't know how it works.

That is a great principle to adhere to; don't invest in something unless you understand the industry in which it functions. Take the time to become familiar with what you want to place your money in and determine beforehand if you can live with yourself if the investment flops. Investing is one of the top ways to generate lasting financial wealth. It is up to you and me to figure out a way to capitalize off of it. If you are like me and want to one day become a serious real estate investor, check out *The Millionaire Real Estate Investor, written* by Gary Keller.

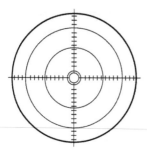

Scope of Accuracy – John C. Bogle

In the investment world, John C. Bogle is considered a giant. In 1974, he founded The Vanguard Group, an investment management company. Bogle grew The Vanguard Group to be the second-largest mutual fund company in the world. He was the visionary who first made the index mutual fund available to the general public when he founded the Vanguard 500 Index Fund. His 10 key rules for investing have enlightened many aspiring entrepreneurs, myself included. Here's a rundown of a few favorites:

- Time is your friend, impulse is your enemy. Take advantage of compound interest and don't be captivated by the allure of the market. That only seduces you into buying after stocks have soared and selling after they plunge.
- Buy right and hold tight. Once you set your asset allocation, stick to it no matter how greedy or scared you become.
- Stay the course. The secret to investing is there is no secret. When you own the entire stock market through a broad stock index fund with an appropriate allocation to an all bond-market index fund, you have the optimal investment strategy. Discipline is best summed up by staying the course.

In 2004, John Bogle was named one of the "world's 100 most powerful and influential people" by Time *magazine. In 1999, Bogle was named one of the investment industry's four "Giants of the 20ᵗʰ Century" by* Fortune *magazine.*

Multiple Streams of Income

I'm probably sure you have heard the term "don't place all your eggs in one basket." That adage couldn't be any truer than the complicated financial times that we are living in now. We are quickly moving away from the era of job security and stability to a more entrepreneurial climate. Even working within a corporation requires an enterprising mindset to be successful. The fact is that we have to all find ways to make extra income outside of our bread and butter methods. What I'm speaking of is creating multiple streams of income. For example, let's say you are a graphics design artist for a Fortune 100 company. Sure, you very well may earn a generous amount of money working for such a prestigious firm, but you understand that competition in the job market is fierce, and you don't what to rest on your laurels and be forced to go without a meal should senior management change their mind about the importance of your role in the company. So you begin to do freelance graphics design on the side. You may not make a ton of money off of this because your main energy is directed toward your regular job.

Nonetheless, you are able to bring in an extra $1,000 a month for your new side venture. You then get the urge to write a book about the stresses and perks associated with being a graphics designer for a Fortune 100 company. You write this book and publish it as an e-book on Amazon, set up a website for it and do light marketing and promotions to get the word out about it. You end up bringing in an extra $200 a month in royalties from Amazon for those curious souls who love your story. Your book piques the interest of the director of the annual graphics designer convention who caught wind of your book on Amazon. She was so moved by your book that she wants to have you as they keynote speaker at this year's convention and offers to pay $500 for your services, in addition to hotel and travel accommodations. You do such a bang-up job at the convention, you begin to get invited to other graphics design conferences and conventions around the country to speak and sign books. The demand for your freelance graphic design skills has also increased exponentially in the process.

Do you see where I'm going with this? You have your first stream of income, which is your job. You were slowly but surely able to add three additional income streams via freelance work, an eBook, and speaking engagements. The book earns you money while you sleep because people are surfing the Web 24 hours a day, seven days a week. The book opened up another world of people to you who valued what you wrote so much that they wanted to hear you teach in person. Do I hear a cha-ching? You may even get to a point where the demand for your non-9-to-5 work gets so high you may eventually leave your job to build your company. You have created multiple steams of income, some you have to physically work on to earn income, some you are able to earn income with passively after the initial creation and marketing.

One of my all-time favorite books on multiple streams of income is a book by the same title written by Robert G. Allen. In *Multiple Streams of Income*, Allen breaks down several potential ways to add different streams of income to your portfolio. One thing I would suggest as you are mulling over adding new streams of income to your financial portfolio is to do things that you are passionate about. Doing things solely for money's sake is a sure way to become burned out. You will wake up every morning excited about life if you're doing things you love and getting paid for it.

Protect What You Work For

Wouldn't you agree that one of the saddest things to hear about is people who were at one time very wealthy who lost everything they worked so hard for? There is story after story of celebrities and high-profile figures who mismanaged their assets and now are dead broke. These stories hit home for me, especially because I am in the music business and it is a tough industry to bounce back from once you have fallen. I love how rapper Kanye West put it in a song that he did with Common. He said, "You be up so high, if you ever fall off, it feel like a plane crash." That's a way of saying that it is very painful to go back to meager circumstances when you have enjoyed the fruits of success.

You and I may never have money like the world's wealthiest entertainers and businesspeople. We can still protect what we do make to ensure that we leave an inheritance for our children's children. The power of accuracy transcends generations. The world is set up in a way to prey on your hard-earned dollars and assets. I believe in paying taxes because that is the price we pay for living in a civilized world. Yet, it is wise to find legal ways of protecting our income and assets; the government is not paid to do that for us. I recommend becoming familiar with estate planning, taxes and insurance if you are not. Estate planning will allow you to distribute your assets to your heirs should something happen to you and hedges them from being overtaxed if it is set up properly.

Keep an eye on what you earn, even if you hire financial professionals to manage your assets. It is smart to have knowledge of what you are employing a specialist to do when it comes to your assets. You want to be able to speak the same language and know whether or not they are misleading you. Most of the great people who lost it all will probably tell you that it was due to them being a little careless and trusting the wrong people. We can prevent many of our financial woes if we are proactive and take the time to learn the information needed to make correct decisions.

Protecting your assets can be a bit of a boring subject if you are not a numbers person. I'm sure you would much rather hear about earning it, but it is pointless to earn more if there is a huge hole in your pocket. One of the biggest reasons to protect your income is so that your loved ones will be taken care of should something happen to you. So give it some thought.

Giving

Generosity is something that is governed by an unseen law and its affects are powerful. The wealthiest and richest people are typically big givers. There is something that unlocks in the spiritual realm when you are generous and give of your treasure. You don't believe me? Let's ask one of the richest and wisest men who ever lived, King Solomon. In his book of wisdom, Proverbs, Solomon confidently asserts, "One man gives freely, yet gains even more; another withholds unduly, but comes to poverty" (Proverbs 11:24, NIV).

It's funny how that works. It sounds like it would be a contradiction to become wealthy by giving more as oppose to holding on to our money and becoming poor. I don't think this wise saying talks about money alone. There is a richness of life that also comes to those who are givers. True wealth is not measured solely by one's financial position. Wealth is a matter of your overall well-being.

> *Estate planning will allow you to distribute your assets to your heirs should something happen to you and hedges them from being overtaxed if it is set up properly.*

The person who gives opens themselves up to the law of abundance. The person who keeps a clenched fist is limited to what they refuse to share.

Jesus Christ stated that it's better to give than to receive (Acts 20:35). That is a weighty statement. The person who is able to give is in a much better position than the one who just receives. Giving is a sign of how well off you are both materially and spiritually. You don't have to be rich to give. As a matter of fact, you absolutely shouldn't wait until you are financially secure before you start to give. Generosity is like a muscle and the more you use it, the more it becomes an integral part of your character.

I know we are talking about finances in this section, But I would like to extend our scope a little bit as it relates to giving. Many times, when we think of giving, we think of charity or just giving money away. Giving is much broader than that. We can also give by offering to others our time, skill sets, brain power, and physical strength. More than anything else, we should seek to help people in their development so they can become givers as well.

An epiphany of sorts came to me a while ago. It is noble to give a man some fish and it is even better to teach him how to fish, but the best thing by far is to show him how to own and manage the lake where the fish dwell. A mature goal for giving is to empower people to be able to do the same for someone else eventually. This principle doesn't just apply to individual people either. When giving to organizations or programs, there should generally be an underlying agenda to help them take care of themselves. There will, of course, be times when we give one time and that's all. However, the true benefit for the receiver is typically obtained when their legs are strengthened so that they can stand on their own.

The people, organizations and institutions that I now give the most to are those that have a mindset to help themselves. In my opinion, these are the ones who really deserve assistance because they aren't trying to mooch their way out of their problems. Giving to people who are not willing to actively participate in changing their circumstances further debilitates them and positively reinforces their negative condition. In those cases, I would advise you to be cautious in how you give.

Keep Greed in Check

Another aspect of giving that should be mentioned is that generosity helps to keep greed in check. It is not hard to get trapped in the rat race of getting more things. If giving is done properly it helps to keep the human tendency of hoarding at bay. Sacrificial giving helps to remind the human mind and spirit that true life is not found in the abundance of possessions. Providing for the wellbeing of others gives life to them and the awareness of true life is awakened in us for having done that. Furthermore, when we give, it should not be done for recognition. The human ego can be very good at trying to reap a reward for anything it does.

An accurate life seeks the reward of making a difference in someone's life, not to get a pat on the back and impress people. There are many people who use fundraisers, charity dinners and banquets for PR opportunities and to further their agenda. This type of giving is disingenuous. It is much more powerful and impactful to quietly mentor someone than to give a million dollars to them for the public to see. Accuracy gives without thought of receiving applause.

Tithing

I want to briefly touch on tithing before we leave from here. Tithing is an ancient Judeo-Christian practice of giving 10 percent of one's income to the church or synagogue. There is a lot of debate today regarding the relevancy of tithing and its place in modern society. I love the way one pastor broke it down, saying that tithing was never for the sake of God. To paraphrase, tithing was for man's benefit so that we are reminded of Him who gives us the ability to earn income. Every time we give a tenth or more, our faith (divine influence from God) is stretched and shows that we value the Blesser more than the blessing. This thought revolutionized my thinking, in terms of why tithing was important. I always thought tithing was for the sole benefit of the church and the pastor (there is some benefit for them and rightly so), but the true benefit lies in keeping a malleable heart toward God in the area of finances.

Often, our giving or lack thereof reveals where our heart is. We typically place the greatest value on whatever allows us to eat. By tithing, we show that we know who the real source of our provision is — God.

Furthermore, God doesn't require a tenth these days. He requires everything. God desires to have the whole person, money included.

Don't Serve Money, Let It Serve You

If I asked most people if they wanted to be rich, the majority would answer yes. Who doesn't want to have abundance? I certainly do and I think it is very obtainable. Yet, there is a trap in pursuing money. If we are not careful, we will fall into it without knowing. Money is a great thing to have, but it must not become what we live for. It is hard to not make money a god in the times we are living in. Everything promotes the worship of money. Accurate lives don't serve money, money serves them.

The only way to not fall into the pit of money worship is to keep God the number one focus and priority of life. A little earlier I stated that our human nature tends to place a high value on whatever feeds us. Money is directly tied to this most basic need. Yet, we must cultivate a deep understanding that God is the one who gives us the ability to earn the money that buys the food we eat. I am very thankful when I have money. It makes things go a lot smoother. I'm not thankful toward money though. I am thankful to God, who graciously provides for me.

The other aspect I want to discuss regarding the servitude of money is learning how to keep money in its proper perspective. Money is a means to an end, not the end itself. People fall in love with money as if it were the air they are breathing. We would find out how valuable money really was if we were alone on a deserted island with no food or shelter. A sandwich made of $100 bills doesn't sound too appealing. People are the ones who create and place value on money. Currency is rapidly changing from paper to other forms such as digital currency. It sounds silly, but we can become so enthralled by these little green sheets of paper that we start believing that they are more than they really are.

With all that said, it behooves you and me to develop a healthy handle on money. Money is a tool that we should all use to further our progress and help others. Today, consumerism has captured the hearts and desires of many people. It has caused them to place rational thought on the shelf (in regards to money) and pursue instant gratification at their own peril. The desire to keep up with the latest and greatest keeps the masses in a perpetual state of financial bondage. In 2014, only 51 percent of Americans had less credit card debt than savings, while China as a whole has become the largest consumer of gold assets. We Americans could sure learn a lot from our Chinese brothers and sisters on how to spend money. Our lust for material wealth turns us into servant s of money. We become slaves to our wants and have to make more and more money to keep up appearances and support a lifestyle most cannot afford.

Become the Lender, Not the Borrower

Accuracy goes against the grain and causes money to work for the earner and not vice versa. There are times when we have to forego instant payoff for long-term benefit. I like what Robert Kiyosaki, author of the acclaimed *Rich Dad Poor Dad*, said on this matter. He stated, "Don't buy luxuries until you have the assets to afford them." I'm all for luxury and the finer things in life, but they must be obtained in the proper sequence to avoid financial slavery.

> *"If you will live like no one else, later you can live like no one else."*
> — *Dave Ramsey*

I'll never forget the very first credit card that I got and how dumb I was with it. It had a $500 limit and I spent $300 of it on a piece of equipment that I hardly ever used after I got it. The worst part was that I didn't have a job so I wasn't able to pay back what I owed once the bill came due. I made minimum payments and then the little bit of money that I was getting dried up. Needless to say, the credit card bill eventually went to collections and my credit score plummeted. I had to fork over my hard-earned cash (whenever I did have a job) to pay back the creditors for something that wasn't a necessity. I learned a very valuable lesson then. I could have saved the money for the piece of equipment that I wanted, invested it and made more than enough money to buy that piece of equipment three times over.

My hunger for instant gratification caused me to make a bad judgment call and it got me off to a bad financial start in life. I had to become a slave to my creditors until I paid my debt back with interest. I was in essence a borrower and my creditors were the lender. King Solomon said, "The rich rule over the poor, and the borrower is slave to the lender" (Proverbs 22:7, NIV). Every time you and I buy something we cannot afford and put it on credit, we are signing up for legalized slavery. Some may think the interest charges we pay are small for the benefit of getting what you want now, but often we are paying more than 30 percent in interest for this shortcut.

It is wiser to figure out a way to earn the money for what you want. If you can't figure out a way to get it, don't obtain it until you can find a way. The things we feel like we can't live without are often trivial and don't keep their luster after we've had them for a month. One wise financial expert said that he only buys luxury items using the interest he gets from his investments. You may not be that hardcore and ready for that type of spending habit, but it is a smart one to keep in your back pocket. Find little ways to reward yourself for reaching your financial goals until you can afford the bigger ones.

To become a lender we must sacrifice for a season. We have to go without some of the comforts of life so that we can sustain a comfortable lifestyle in the future. Dave Ramsey often states, "If you will live like no one else, later you can live like no one else." Make up your mind to become the person in good financial standing so that one day it will be a reality for you. Imagine how great that would feel, to own your home, cars, clothes and "toys" free and clear. Imagine being able to take vacations on your own dime when you want. Imagine paying for your children's education outright with no financial obligation after the fact. Feels great doesn't it? Well, it is possible if you do the ground work today.

Final Thought on Finances

We've briefly discussed a lot of information on the broad subject of finances. The goal wasn't to answer all questions but to provide a holistic view of how to be accurate in this area. I recommend that you take the subject of finances very seriously and try to master it. Financial matters are highly important and those who go through the pains of understanding them will be much better off in life. Many well intentioned people don't take the time to learn how money works and deceive themselves into thinking that everything will all just pan out. Nothing could be further from the truth. It is our own responsibility to educate ourselves and learn how to earn, retain and make money work for us.

Be cautious about what type of information you take in concerning finances. It is wise to confirm the information you get with several other sources before you make a life-altering decision. The most accurate information will be widely recognized and you should be able to find a pattern in what is presented if it is reputable. I am continually reading new and old books on finances to stay sharp in this area and to develop a healthy bank of knowledge to draw from.

As we conclude this chapter, I want you to reflect on your overall values that I had you list earlier because these will help you stay in line with your financial goals. It takes planning and strategy to come out on top financially. Accurately managing your finances does not have to be complicated or difficult. On the contrary, you want to keep it as simple as possible so that you can make it a lifelong habit.

Application of Accuracy

- **Create a budget.**
- **Review your budget regularly.**
- **Save up seed money for investing.**
- **Learn how to make money work for you.**

CHAPTER 8

Occupation

You've probably heard the saying, "If you do what you love then you'll never work another day in your life." While I do believe that is true to a certain degree, I do think that there are aspects of a dream occupation that prove difficult and tedious as well. The goal of this section is to present some thoughts on how accurate minds approach occupation. We want to find ourselves doing what we love because it makes it that much easier to face the inevitable obstacles that come from earning a living in this world.

Much of who we are is defined by what kind of work we do. For some reason, this is just the way our society is wired. We tend to define people by their occupation. Occupation is not the "end all be all" of who a person is, but it does reveal a lot. Therefore, it is an important aspect of life and deserves some attention. A lot of people consider work to be a burden. How many times have you heard or thought to yourself, "I wish I didn't have to work?" While most of us feel this way from time to time, work is a gift from God and it gives us a sense of purpose, dignity and accomplishment.

A Reality Check

When I was in my early twenties, I remember having a conversation with my older cousin about moving back to California as well as my goals and plans related to music. I remember telling him that my plan was not to work a regular job, but to pursue music full time. I was convinced that this plan would work. My cousin just listened patiently and then at the end of my heartfelt and passionate discourse he told me bluntly that I needed to find a job. My bubble busted and my ego was a little bruised. But in retrospect, I should have paid him for these truthful words.

I was living in a dream world. I was very young and naïve and thought that I could take the world by storm without earning the right to do so. I didn't really know how the world operated. Success comes with hard work that is at times unpleasant. Success in any endeavor is more difficult than we anticipate and requires sacrifice to make it come about. His advice was not for me to give up on my dreams of being a world-famous musician, but to be practical and make sure I was doing something to take care of my basic needs in the meantime. Today, I am able to do what I love because I made the initial steps of setting up a base to operate from as I pursued my true calling.

Everyone's story is different. Perhaps you are able to go after your dreams without giving any thought to much of anything else. Great for you! But this story is just to illustrate the importance of developing and maintaining a mindset to work no matter what position you find yourself in. People who are living their dream will often tell you that there is an immense amount of work that goes on behind the scenes that most people don't see. Michael Jordan didn't become arguably the greatest basketball player that ever lived because of sheer talent alone. He put in the work necessary to become the dominant athlete that he was. Jordan became the most intimidating force in the NBA by putting in long hours and training beyond what average superstars usually did. He showed extreme accuracy in his occupation and we can take that same mentality into our own professions.

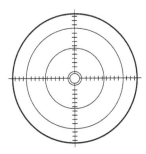

Scope of Accuracy – Michael Jordan

Michael Jeffrey Jordan is not only a basketball icon; he has become a symbol of greatness that transcends the confines of the athletic world. Simply put, Michael Jordan has become the definition of what it means to be the best in any arena. The six-time NBA champion, five-time NBA MVP, 10-time All-NBA First Team, nine-time All-Defensive First Team, and 14-time All Star has demonstrated accuracy both on and off the court.

Jordan has parlayed his likeness into the world-renowned Jordan brand. He has had endorsement deals with Hanes, Ball Park Franks, Wheaties, Gatorade and many more. Jordan became the majority owner of the Charlotte Bobcats (formerly the Hornets) in 2010. He was named the first NBA player to become a billionaire in June 2014. Jordan's popularity and relevance is still unmatched, according to a 2013 ESPN Sports poll.

Jordan's love for his chosen occupation of basketball is somewhat of a phenomenon. Various coaches, teammates and critics alike have said Jordan wants to win more than anyone else. His fire to succeed has carried him to unprecedented heights that won't be forgotten anytime soon. Below are some of Jordan's principles on success:

- *Be the first to arrive at practice and the last to leave.*
- *Don't be afraid to try. You can never succeed without the possibility of failure.*
- *Use pain as motivation.*
- *Let your game do the talking for you.*
- *Limits like fears are often just illusions.*

Doing the Grunt Work First

One of my favorite Proverbs reads, "Finish your outdoor work and get your fields ready; after that, build your house" (Proverbs 24:27, NIV). In order to reap the benefits of accuracy, one has to be willing to do the work that is not applauded at first. That may mean enduring boring trainings, filling out tedious paperwork, studying, filling an undesirable entry-level position, creating a business plan or whatever else may be necessary to get to the prime objective. These little unseen things are often what ensure success in one's occupation.

In our hyper-fast "give it to me now" culture, many aim for the C-suite without first developing their character in the mailroom. To overcome this, we have to let go of our sense of entitlement. The world doesn't owe us anything. Once we've learned this, it will transform the way we approach our job, especially the tasks for which we think we're overqualified.

We will often find that we are better off going through the pains of earning our success. I am much more appreciative of the platforms and doors that open up to me after I have worked my way up to them. The whole time I am doing grunt work, I keep my overall goal before me so that I don't lose perspective while working toward it.

In my younger days, I remember hearing the story of another author whose book went on to be a huge success. She said one of her biggest regrets, in hindsight, was that she did not plan for success. When she put out her book, the response was so overwhelming that her website crashed several times from all the traffic and she didn't have enough supply for her clients' demand. Although I can't recall her name, her story left an indelible mark on me even at that age. The lesson I learned was to get my fields ready, which means plan for success.

Accuracy makes room for success. Those who are successful may not have attained it in their earlier occupations, positions or endeavors but they always did their due diligence to ensure would have a better success ratio down the road. Any job or position that I've ever failed at was typically due to me not planning for success in one way or another. We plan for success by building an infrastructure that can hold up under the demand that success brings.

Training

The great philosophical mind Aristotle once said, "Excellence is an art won by training and habituation. We do not act rightly because we have virtue or excellence, but we rather have those because we have acted rightly. We are what we repeatedly do. Excellence, then, is not an act but a habit."

> *We plan for success by building an infrastructure that can hold up under the demand success brings.*

In any occupation, we should commit ourselves to continual training. Our minds grow dull if we aren't actively perfecting our skillfulness. It is astounding how, after training in a certain area, a fiery interest can grow for something that we didn't initially care about. Undergoing training causes us to invest in our current occupations and we sense even greater ownership of them. You may be in a job that you hate, but you will find yourself beginning to enjoy it a little more if you invest some time in becoming better at it each day.

In grade school I hated math and I was never really any good at it. Part of the reason why is because I didn't study (train) as I needed to before a test or quiz. There was typically a sense of dread that accompanied me when I went to math class. Yet, when I studied adequately and went to tutoring, I looked forward to class and was much more engaged while there. Continual training and preparation renews lost vigor or produces it if there was very little to begin with.

Promotion is generally tied to our attitude about our current position and our attitudes are often directly related to our training. Become accurate in what is assigned to you, even if you aren't crazy about it and you are much more likely to be given a responsibility that you enjoy later. Training enables you to become accurate and it is not just useful in your current occupation, it is something that betters you as a person if you find a way to use it.

Passion

I'm going to take a back door approach as we dive into the topic of passion. Instead of the popular notion of pursuing your passion (which I am also a believer in), I would like to present the idea of turning what you currently do into your passion. The hard truth is that many of us will have jobs that we don't like until we are in a position to do what we love. These pre-occupations are good character and skill-development tools that will serve us well when we actually get to fill our dream occupations. Cal Newport, author of *So Good They Can't Ignore You*, postulates that we stumble into our passion by doing things that we don't care for initially.

A key to accuracy in your occupation is to discover how what you are doing now will benefit what you plan to do later. It is much easier to give our all to something that we feel is a stepping stone rather than a dead end. The beauty in this thought is that there is always something in whatever we are currently doing that will help prepare us for our true passion. For example, Brent plans to one day be the mayor of his city. He has a knack for people and what it takes to create positive change in every sphere of influence that he has found himself in. But before he can move into this position, he has to graduate from college first.

Brent doesn't come from a wealthy background, so he has to work to pay his way through school. He lands a respectable job as a warehouse associate at Office Depot. This is definitely not his dream. Yet Brent has an accurate mindset and decides to give his all to this job. He learns the importance of being punctual, how to work well with colleagues and superiors, and how to go above and beyond what is asked of him. He also takes time to learn about the company he works for and those who hold senior management positions at his location. He doesn't do this to jockey for position, but to develop a stronger sense of ownership for his position and workplace. He sees beyond just driving pallet jacks, wrapping pallets and moving boxes. He is learning transferrable skills of integrity, hard work, leadership, interpersonal skills and consistency, which are all non-negotiable traits for a mayor.

He demonstrates quiet leadership and does so without a title. His co-workers respect him and senior management notices something different about him. Brent has found a way to link his overall passion with his current occupation. The sky is the limit for this type of mind, let alone the office of mayor.

From this example, we all can learn not to become fixated on not being where we want to be. Rather, we capitalize on every ounce of training (both informal and formal) available to us in our current occupation, and find creative ways to "make" ourselves passionate about it and gain invaluable expertise, all the while keeping our eyes set on our future destination. That is powerful stuff and that is accurate living demonstrated at its finest in the realm of occupation.

Expertise

One of my favorite pearls of wisdom is, "Do you see a man skilled in his work? He will serve before kings; he will not serve before obscure men" (Proverbs 22:29, NASB). Expertise is our developed skill, knowledge and execution combined. There is a great chance that our expertise will be honored by people of influence if we remain consistent, keeping both a great attitude and excellent performance. In the Bible, we see that Joseph the dreamer was promoted in every place he worked because of his expertise in administration as well as his ability to interpret dreams.

You and I both have a specific niche to fill. Expert status doesn't come over night; it is earned over the course of several years. Malcolm Gladwell, author of the bestseller *Outliers*, mentions that it takes 10,000 hours of dedicated practice to achieve mastery in one's profession. There is some debate around this; however, most of the greats in their respective fields will tell you that practice is essential to mastery, if that's even possible. Some people develop their expertise sooner than others but there is always a process. We need to find our lane of expertise in our occupations to be accurate in the workplace. Usually we will have to give up other things to become great at others, but the rewards of this sacrifice are worth their weight in gold.

We have to be willing to give our all to whatever we are focusing on in order to see big results. It is hard to not be a jack of all trades these days. I'm not suggesting that we should put all of our economic eggs in one basket, yet we should choose an occupation that we can immerse ourselves. On this solid foundation, we will be able to diversify into other areas because we have mastered the one we started with. There will be circumstances that arise in life where you have to "hustle" and come up with something quick to make ends meet; however, it is not wise to make this the norm. It is a much more fulfilling and profitable arrangement to zero in on occupations that we are interested in that may grow into passion. Accuracy will cause us to go after that which has lasting value, not just temporary gain.

I learned a great deal from a gentleman by the name of Mark Jewell, who was one of my instructors for a class I was taking for my job. He continued to drive home the importance of picking a specific industry and sticking with it. Those who jump around from industry to industry will never be successful. That concept makes me think of very old trees that have been around for hundreds of years. Oftentimes, their roots grow longer than what we see above ground. It would be impossible for these huge trees to thrive if someone constantly uprooted them and put them in another climate.

We can grow to be giants in our occupations if we stay in them long enough. We will inadvertently become experts and influential people will find value in us. Seth Godin is a favorite business thought leader of mine. He points out, "The secret to being the best in the world is to make the world smaller."

Work Ethic

You may have heard the witty saying, "The only time success comes before work is in the dictionary." These are words to live by as it relates to occupation. Our road to accuracy in the vocational environment is our strong work ethic. Your commitment to give your best every day is what will set you apart in your endeavors and ultimately lead to your success. It's funny how the simplest truths regarding success are ignored. It is human nature to travel the road of least resistance. In other words, it's inherent for all of us to be lazy.

So many people give into this destructive trait by cloaking it with the mask of busyness. Now, more than ever it is easy to give our attention to everything except what we should focus our energies on. It's much easier to feel productive than to actually be productive. Hard work is, well, hard. Part of that hard work nowadays is related to staying focused and not giving into the gravitational pull of surface level productivity.

We must be willing to consistently invest our time, energy, mental capacity and even our financial resources into what we are pursuing. There are several different factors that contribute to vocational success, but work ethic is the granddaddy of them all. Every position that I've done well in could be traced back to the launching pad called "the grind." Your drive is what will generate your desired result. The time in which we live does not promote this line of thinking. It often seems that the spin of today's media is to focus our attention on the one in a million or the meteoric rise of someone famous. This produces a false notion that success comes easily. We see people who seemingly have equal or lesser talent than us on larger platforms. All the while, we are not aware of what put that person in their current position.

Accuracy teaches us that our fortunes lie buried under the timeless principles of determination, perseverance, focus, and work. Accurate lives work hard on the things that matter and tend to brush off the things that glitter but are far from gold. I am inspired by the work ethic of many entrepreneurs that I have witnessed in the Korean-American community. I've been in several of their family owned businesses and have seen every employee pour their best effort into whatever assignment they are given. The CEOs and presidents of these companies are typically the hardest workers in their firms.

I was intrigued by the work ethic of the Korean-Americans whom I had encountered so I begin to do a little research on how they developed it. It turns out that many of the first-generation Korean-Americans came to the United States in hope for a better life but could not find work or were forced to do back-breaking labor that paid below minimum wage. In order to overcome this, many became entrepreneurs in order to provide a good life for their children and grandkids. They place a high value on education and many Korean-American parents work strenuous hours in order to fund their children's education. I also discovered that the racism and other obstacles they faced in this country caused them to remain a tight-knit community in support for one another. You often see Korea towns or entire business districts dominated by these resilient people.

I once went into a fast food restaurant that was owned by a Korean-American woman and she worked harder than all of her staff. She did everything from working the cash register, to cooking the fries, to greeting guests, and brining their food to them. I was impressed by her work ethic. On top of that, she worked 12 hours a day, seven days a week. I'm not necessarily suggesting we all adopt that same schedule and work routine, but there is something to glean from this young woman. She has a "by any means necessary" attitude to succeed in her occupation, and she has really taken her future into her own hands by buying a business and working it.

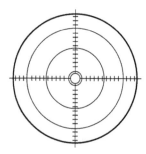

Scope of Accuracy – South Korea

South Korea is a country with a rich legacy. The struggles that Koreans have faced and overcome has instilled in them a work ethic and drive for excellence that is unparalleled. The country suffered devastation after the Korean War and one-third of the population became homeless. However, the

Korean people have such a deep passion for education and advancement that their universities would set up tents to hold lectures.

Another fundamental quality of Koreans that sets them apart is the importance they place on the group. In business, Koreans see the success of a company as a reflection of the entire group, not just one superstar CEO. Korean CEOs don't have the same high salaries and stock option plans that American CEOs do.

Koreans believe in constant innovation. Proof of this is seen in Korean companies, such as Samsung, whom takes an already great product and modifies it to be even better. On an individual level, you will find Korean elders learning how to speak different languages in their latter years. Middle-aged Koreans often take additional vocational classes after they have earned their degree in order to move ahead at work. It's the importance they place on education, sense of community over individualism, and the pursuit of mastery that allows many Koreans to be successful in the United States and abroad.

Becoming Invaluable

In your lifetime you've probably seen people who are great at what they do but they can be really arrogant about it. These are the personalities that people hate to compliment because it just inflates their egos even more. If we are not careful, the accuracy that we consciously demonstrate can produce the same trait in us. Becoming invaluable to those we serve in our occupations is accomplished by being excellent in our work performance while maintaining a pleasant attitude. Arrogance is a stench that attracts flies to our best efforts.

We should gracefully carry confidence in our abilities while simultaneously keeping a sense of our frailties. A humble attitude and accurate performance will go a long way in any endeavor. Our goal should be to let our work speak for its self rather than toot our own horn. Invaluable people don't have to speak highly of themselves to others; there is a line of people waiting to do that for them.

Some of the best advice that I got was from a young lady who really enjoys my music. She told me not to get caught up in the hype, but to keep my head down, focus and continue to work on my vision. I have taken this wisdom to heart and try to incorporate this in my day-to-day operations. Developing the habit of valuable consistent performance will not go unrecognized forever. Don't fall for the temptation of unwarranted self-promotion. A quiet and productive worker will always outshine a loud and unproductive one.

Accuracy places the greatest importance on results, even if we don't get the credit for it. There are eyes watching you at every moment and the people that make a difference will see your value. So let's add value and not pine after the limelight. If it comes, great, and if not, that works even better sometimes. The work that takes place under the surface of a fruit tree makes what is seen possible.

Avoid Workplace Politics

The first job that I landed after college was for a startup entrepreneurial venture that was very promising. It was a family owned operation. Working there was a great experience for me because I got my first dose of workplace politics. Some managers and employees would try to outshine, outwit and strategically position themselves. There were those in the company who stayed out of such scheming, but there were several that engaged in it.

> *Accuracy places the greatest importance on results, even if we don't get the credit for it.*

I tried, for a time, to play the game. But I just wasn't any good at it. I never had the make-up needed to be deceptive or manipulative. I would feel like a sleaze bag if I employed those methods for any length of time. I opted to just work hard and focus on being the best employee I could. I already had some familial clout with the owner of the company. Therefore, I had something working in my favor beyond just my personal drive. I decided to couple this favor with a unique and honest work ethic. After 18 months on the job, I received a substantial promotion and raise; seven months later I was promoted again.

Instead of working the angles (which I was no good at), I decided not to get caught up in the "he said, she said" that went on at work. I would keep my ears open to important information, but other than that I didn't participate in the water cooler talk too much. In my mind, the time spent trying to play politics could be used to get work done.

As I mentioned earlier, accuracy places the greatest importance on results. People who use politics to advance will only have short-term success in their careers, if any. Wherever there are two or more people, there will be politics. But we do not have to play by those rules. It is much better for us to keep our focus on delivering results consistently, building relationships and operating in integrity.

There is a Machiavellian mentality that pervades most work environments. This mindset encourages us to manipulate our way to the top, make friends with the right people, flex power and feign submission to superiors. This mode of thinking is cancerous and disrupts real progress. I'm all for being strategic and pensive, but these traits should only be used to produce the most beneficial result for all parties involved, even if we get the short end of the stick. Workplace politics is a dangerous game to play no matter what industry you are in and it always causes division. Not to mention, we will be more prone to losing peace of mind and sleep at night when we are not taking secure paths to vocational success.

Most people dislike the antics used by many politicians to obtain their offices, so our standard should be the same in our specific work place. We must stay away from negative talk and from spreading misinformation. At the end of the day, we want our reputations to be what causes us to be promoted and not the working of angles. If we focus on delivering great results in integrity, we will have fewer headaches and not fear our dirty laundry being aired (since we have none or have already aired it ourselves).

Accept the Challenges That No One Else Will

One of the greatest ways to set ourselves apart in the workplace is to accept challenging assignments that most others shun. We provide our greatest value when we solve complicated problems and are able to articulate the solution we found. Embracing tough assignments is the mark of a leader, and it shows that we are willing to go into uncharted and seemingly dangerous territory. Not only do we want to accept these challenges, we also want to excel in them. Should we fail, we want to leave no doubt in the minds of our co-workers that there was no stone left unturned as we tried to accomplish the assignment.

The better we get at accepting and solving problems, the more comfortable we will be with uncertainty. Years of honing and refining accuracy in our occupations will shine through eventually with powerful results. I once heard someone say that leaders are forged during times of crisis. Some of the greatest CEOs and businesspeople of our times are those who took on a challenge that no one else wanted anything to do with. Take Lee Iacocca for example. In the late 1970s he agreed to become president and CEO of Chrysler Corporation when it was on its way out of business. There probably wasn't a long line for that position. I'm sure even the most seasoned and successful CEOs of that time thought he was foolish for making a move like that. Yet, Iacocca was able to turn the company around within seven years. That "crazy" decision to accept a challenge that no else wanted would place him on an international platform.

With all that said, we should know which challenges we have a shot at and the ones that are out of our league at the moment. Iacocca's decision to head the failing automobile company was calculated and he was well aware of the ramifications if he failed. He already had a track record in leading a major automobile company and he demonstrated the acumen necessary for what he would face at Chrysler. It would not be advisable for someone to try to fix a large company's information technology problem if they don't even know how to fix a virus on their personal computer. Let us be wise and count the cost before we leap out to tackle anything in our work environments.

If nothing else, we should be able to live with ourselves if the challenge gets the best of us and we don't succeed in what we attempted. Our resilience in temporary failure is a great indicator of whether or not we should take on certain risks. Is taking the promotion within that egotistical division going destroy my sense of self-worth should I fail in it? Will I be able to bounce back if upper management rejects this proposal I have spent the last three months working on? Can I handle the criticism of my co-workers if this new marketing concept that I helped develop flops? These are the types of questions we need to ask ourselves before we swim into the shark-infested waters of risk and challenge. We will find that we have a greater chance of success if we are well aware of what we are getting ourselves into, we have a plan for how to handle what we will face, and we have a track record in the given area of challenge we are taking on.

Application of Accuracy

- Plan for success by doing the necessary grunt work first. Build your infrastructure of knowledge, contacts and other resources needed.
- Engage in continual training in your occupation. Keep your passion alive.
- Put in the necessary work to rise to the top.
- Avoid workplace politics.
- Become invaluable
- Accept challenges that no one else will.

CHAPTER 9

Business and Entrepreneurship

One of the chief reasons that I wrote this book was out of a desire to convey what successful people are doing that sets them apart from those who are not. The idea morphed into something that includes every important category of human life. But at its core, there is a hunger to know how to build successful companies, organizations and other entrepreneurial ventures. I was blessed to have a job that forced me to get out of my comfort zone and go into several different communities and speak with businesspeople from all walks of life. I've met highly successful businesspeople to humble mom-and-pop companies barely making the rent to keep the doors open. Regardless of what state these entrepreneurial businesses were in, I loved the fact that someone had the guts to step out and build something on their own.

I truly believe that entrepreneurship is one of the most creative undertakings in existence. With it, we have the opportunity to take our financial destinies into our own hands, create new markets and jobs, build wealth, and help improve the world through our products, services and overall influence. For the past several years I have studied, researched and written about entrepreneurship and top-notch entrepreneurs on my blog, Rebelfirm.com. Truth be told, this part could probably be a book of its own due to my passion for it, but for now we will discuss it briefly. Let this chapter inspire you as you seek accuracy in this area.

Learn How to Fail Well

Almost any entrepreneur will tell you that failure is bound to happen at some time or another on the journey toward greatness. Tom Szaky, founder and CEO of TerraCycle, put it like this: "The truth is, all success is built on failure." Failure is just the tuition we all pay for the school of success. I thought it would be important to start the chapter with this thought because the message widely marketed to us today is that success should be instantaneous. I've seen so many people throw in the towel in some very promising pursuits because results didn't come quick enough. I once heard someone say that it takes seven to 10 years to become truly proficient at something. Nowadays, most people are on a six week proficiency plan. There are certain processes that we can't take shortcuts on no matter how fast we move.

Building a business is hard and it takes more than just a good idea for it to flourish. One of my favorite sayings that I've heard is, "life is a marathon." The same is true for building a long-lasting enterprise. We have to become OK with the fact that we will fail from time to time. If we keep running our race, we will eventually see the fruits of our labor. There is a huge difference between failing and being a failure. Failing is just part of the learning curve. We only become failures when we give up. Several successful entrepreneurs who I have read about cited perseverance as being one of the chief traits that led to their success. It's the ability to overcome the negative emotions we feel after we fail, then continue onward that separates winners from losers.

> *There is a huge difference between failing and being a failure. Failing is just part of the learning curve. We only become failures when we give up.*

Our humanity produces natural inconsistencies; not to mention, we have gifts inside us that have to be developed. As we build companies, these are two very important things to keep in mind. On top of that, we have to learn our markets and have to give those within our markets time to trust who we are and what we offer them. The popular term for this is called branding. There are definitely going to be some times when we drop the ball as we are trying to juggle all of the different aspects of entrepreneurship. I'm a proponent of the school of thought that believes creating a business is a calling and not just a job. It makes it a little easier to fail and keep at it if you're doing something you have given your life to.

The key in failing well is to not give up no matter what. We must tell ourselves daily that we will not quit. I cringe at the thought of giving up on my businesses and living with the "what ifs." Our perspectives have to change on how we look at failing. Experience is usually earned through trial and error. Being an expert at something just means that a person failed the most and eventually got it right. He or she failed enough times to know what not to do the next time around. People will eventually pay for our failures if we hang in the fight long enough to change our fate. We usually only pay attention to the current status of the people we admire. We typically gloss right over the parts of their biographies where they cite their failures. Jim Carrey, one of the greatest comedians and entertainers of our time, was booed off stage the first time he attempted comedy. He came from a hard upbringing, often having to sleep in a van with his family. Carrey honed his craft by performing for his mom, who was very sick at the time, making her laugh so she would get better. In my opinion, there aren't too many entertainers that can match Carrey's talent, yet even he had to fail first. His journey was no bed of rose pedals. On the contrary, we get to appreciate his gifts because of what he suffered initially.

We don't want to give up on the enterprises in our hearts and 20 or 30 years down the road look back and say I wonder where I would be right now had I just gotten over my fear of failure and kept moving. Even if we didn't necessarily end up in the position we expected to be in, we would be a lot closer and probably a lot more successful if we had not given up. An archer who continues to shoot arrows will eventually hit the bull's eye. It's OK to fail when you have a continual desire to learn and improve.

Failing well includes contemplation. We need to reflect on what went wrong and what we plan to do differently the next time around. It's sort of like moving through a maze. We are able to pinpoint where the dead ends are the next time around because we already bumped into those walls. Perhaps next time we can take a different route and see what happens. This type of perspective is energizing and turns our failings into valuable information for the next round. Imagine years and years of cultivating this type of mentality and how powerful that would be. We would be so much sharper and better equipped as we entered the boxing ring of entrepreneurship once again.

There should even be reflection after things have gone right. Most people don't ask themselves what could've been done better and what did we execute correctly. For example, if we were to tweak this small thing in our operations it may yield better results in this area. Quality information that is retained is very valuable. As a matter of fact, there are companies that pay millions of dollars to properly manage this information. It's one of the most valuable assets anyone can have.

What Would You Give Your Life To?

Late Apple Inc. CEO Steve Jobs was someone who wanted to build a company that could change the world — he just happened to make computers. It is not enough just to create something; there should be a larger reason behind what we are doing. Accurate entrepreneurs are those who use their products and services as a platform to communicate a much greater idea. There is generally a passion that drives them beyond the sole desire to make a bunch of money. Money, believe it or not, is not enough of a motivator to stick with something long term. There are many successful executives who would jump at the chance to do their passion. We all have a desire to make a difference and live fulfilling lives.

If you venture out to build a company, it needs to be related to something that you can give your life to. With that said, many of the businesses that we see are very much revenue driven. You have to make a profit to stay in business. There is a beautiful balance that is struck between an entrepreneur who finds a way to make their company profitable and sustainable, as well as make an impact in its given industry. Challenges like this are what get most business owners out of their bed every morning. It's fun to make money; it's an even more rewarding experience to affect positive change in your niche of society.

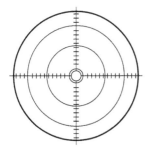

Scope of Accuracy – Jeff Bezos

Jeff Bezos has changed the world through his company, Amazon.com. Named one of America's Best Leaders by US News and World Report, Bezos has reinvented the shopping experience for today's consumer. Bezos believes in three key tenets pertaining to success: *Think long term, make the customer the center of your universe, and invent. These are the pillars that Amazon.com stands on today.*

Bezos is an optimist who affirms that big things start small, which is why he is a strong proponent of long-term thinking. His passion for reading, software and computers is what afforded him the opportunity to blend the Internet (then in its infant stages) with book retail. While the largest brick-and-mortar book stores could hold only about 200,000 titles in house, Amazon.com was able to hold millions of selections in its online catalog. Amazon.com shares rose by 70 percent in 2011.

According to Bezos, it's more important to be customer-focused than competitor-focused. This aspiration is what Bezos hopes Amazon's legacy will be. Bezos himself believes there are no shortcuts. You must go step by step, ferociously. Harvard Business Review *named Bezos the world's second-best CEO, after Steve Jobs, in 2014.*

Your Business Is an Extension of You

Paul Hawken, author of *Growing a Business*, presented an interesting paradigm in his tremendously informative book. He believes that an entrepreneur's business is an extension of who they are. He postulates that it should grow organically out of them. In business school, most students are taught about business and marketing plans, company financials and forecasts. Business often has a metal ring to it.

There is a need for business plans, forecasts and the other usual suspects in launching a business. However, these things are not as important as having a true passion for what you do. Most of us will commit ourselves to our personal welfare. If your business is an outgrowth of who you are, there is an increased likelihood that you will give your all to it because it won't be viewed as a separate entity.

We are able to create our own niche when we build companies that originate in our hearts. I've never been a fan of starting a company simply for the money. We see and hear of many money-driven entrepreneurs in Silicon Valley who start and build companies simply with the goal of selling them to get rich. Many of the venture capitalists who invest in businesses are tired of this type of business model. World-class author and venture capitalist Guy Kawasaki has said that he doesn't seek to invest in companies that are built with the sole goal of being sold. Oftentimes, companies that buy entrepreneurial ventures retain the former CEO to run it. This is because the former CEO's knowledge and passion for what they created is unparalleled.

It is much harder to sell or let go of something if it's connected to you. Of course, we don't want to be dogmatic and never sell our companies if the right opportunity comes along; there is a time and a place for everything. What I am saying is that this option should form organically and not be the goal from the outset. That sounds more like pimping than entrepreneurship!

I am truly inspired by screenwriter and playwright Tyler Perry and his story about refusing to give up on the first play that he wrote. He spent thousands of hard-earned dollars putting together this stage play in his early days. He lost a lot of money in this venture during the course of several years, often performing the plays before a small audience of people he knew personally. Yet, Perry couldn't give up on his vision because it was too intertwined with who he was. He eventually became successful and now has a net worth of about $350 million because of his persistence. The empire that he has created came out of his heart. You would be hard pressed to disassociate his company from him as a person.

There is no way that Perry could have walked away from himself. Similarly there was no way that he could have walked away from his company because it would have been like amputating an arm. Accurate entrepreneurs are those who build enterprises that are a part of them. It is hard for these types of endeavors to fail. The only way they cannot succeed is if the entrepreneur gives up on him or herself.

Consistency

In business, just as in life, there is an incredible power that comes with consistency. Eighty percent of the battle is won by just showing up to work every day. Nothing can truly move forward or change without the presence of the visionary of the company. Similarly, the owner of the business sets the tone for the entire organization. If they are inconsistent, volatile and swayed by the wind, the rest of the organization will follow suit.

It's hard to stick with something when the initial excitement is gone or if it produces minimal results. Tyler Perry had only 30 people in the crowd for his first stage production that he spent a hard-earned $12,000 to produce — before he acquired wealth. He forecasted that 200 people would be there. Not only that, he saw the same painful results for about another six years until he finally saw a breakthrough in his production. Yet Perry's consistency and his unwavering faith kept him on course during those dark periods.

We must develop the same mindset if we are to be accurate in our places of business. We must become good at continuing to swing our axes until the tree of entrepreneurial success falls in our favor. There is no way we can sustain a successful enterprise before the public if we have not developed commitment to our business endeavor in private.

Consistency is doing what we needs to be done, even when we don't feel like it. A person who is able to drag their self to the office day in and day out and plug away at their goals will ultimately become successful.

> *There is no way we can sustain a successul enterprise before the public if we have not developed commitment to our business endeavor in private.*

The hidden treasure of consistency is that it also causes you to become better. The longer you do something; you will inadvertently become a pro at it.

The Little Things Make It Easier for the Big Things to Happen

When I was recording my second album, *The Campaign*, someone gave me a great piece of advice that has stuck with me to this day. They told me that it's the little things that ultimately make us successful. There was a time in my life when I would put so much energy into creating a phenomenal product and it couldn't take on a life of its own simply because I procrastinated in doing the small stuff. When you put out an album, it is important to file copyrights, register the music with performing rights societies, and fill out other documents that make it an official release.

I took this part of the job lightly and, as a result, didn't maximize some really great projects. I learned that doing the small things make it easier for the big things to succeed. It's often stated that "the devil is in the details." I'd like to reword that by stating that "accuracy is in the details." The little things in building a business require a great deal of discipline. Developing the habit of handling behind-the-scenes work makes what we put on display so much more potent, valuable and long lasting.

Accurate entrepreneurs understand that doing little things is needed to keep the enterprise successful. It would be unfortunate to build a first-rate restaurant only to have it shut down months later because someone in management overlooked a small food handler's requirement, ultimately causing the business to fail inspection. Think of the little things as the building's foundation, and if they aren't in place, the building will not stand no matter how impressive the architectural design is.

Build the Right Team

Great entrepreneurs know how to build great teams around them. There is hardly anything of significance that you can get done by yourself. We have to find partners who can help take our companies to places that we can't on our own. Perhaps you are a skillful salesperson but lack experience in engineering, which may be something you need to close bigger deals. Find an engineer who loves your business concept and make him or her one of the partners in the company. Add someone who is a marketing expert who can cast a broader net to your specific client base and make them a partner as well. Hunt down a skillful lawyer looking for something exciting to be a part of and add them to the roster. I'm only using this as an example, but I've actually seen a business team such as this assembled.

John C. Maxwell, author of *The 17 Indisputable Laws of Teamwork*, speaks about the law of multiplication. He affirms that an organization can only go so far if the leader is the greatest member within it. The law of multiplication takes the lid off an organization's potential because the leader has taken the time to pour herself into others, making them just as effective as she is, if not more. We want to adopt the same mindset as we build our companies. We don't want to try to juggle every position, but we should intentionally surround

> *Passion is what gets you to the door and causes you to keep walking once you enter through it, but business acumen shows you how to open the door and how to walk through it.*

ourselves with people who are skillful and will help us take the further than we can on our own.

There was a time when the ancient leader of Israel, Moses, was getting burned out because he was carrying all the pressures of governing a nation. He was the sole leader of the newly freed Hebrew nation, which scholars say included more than 2 million people. Talk about responsibility. The buck stopped with him for everything, even the petty squabbles that were unworthy of his time. This is probably one of the reasons why he was so frustrated toward the end of his career. His father-in-law, Jethro, gave him some sage advice and told him to gather around him a leadership team of men who had wisdom, integrity, and a heart for the nation. Moses did as he was instructed and it took a major load off of him.

We, too, can learn a lot from Moses. It is important for us to develop the people around us who are captivated by what we are doing and who are skillful in their own right. As I stated earlier in the book, there are people whose entire vision is a component of yours. We need to find them, bring them into the fold and release them. That way, we can concentrate on the most important things, such as the direction of the business, innovation, and the continued success of our companies.

Create Something You Love and Fortify Your Acumen

Accuracy in business is usually derived from creating something that we are so passionate about that there is no way we can let it fail. Natural momentum is produced when we pour our all into what we are creating. We can't help but try to make it successful in the market or find who can. The difficulty is typically found in creating something that you love and it being something that people will pay for. It can be tricky, but I truly believe that if you're driven by what you create and stick with it, there is a market for what you offer. The market may be obscure and hard to find at first, but your passion will eventually pull your target audience in your direction. There are close to 7 billion people on the planet. I'm sure you can capture a percentage who wants what you have to offer.

With that said, it is critical to not only hone our creativity, but also our business acumen. Think of it like this: It takes more than love to stay married. It also takes more than love to make your business successful in the market. It is definitely the fuel, but it takes an engaged mind to bring together the necessary pieces that make success possible. Most people get it wrong; they believe that their passion will open all the doors for them.

Passion is what gets you to the door and causes you to keep walking once you enter through it, but business acumen shows you *how* to open the door and *how* to walk through it.

I've seen many passionate people fail in their ventures because they relied solely on their love of what they were doing. I learned early on that my love of something must be channeled into me developing the discipline to take it as far as it can possibly go. One of the hardest parts of being an entrepreneur is getting our hearts and our minds to work together. We either see people blinded by passion without the slightest clue of what they're doing, or we see people emotionally detached from what they produce and discard it on a whim. Imagine how rewarding it would be to become an entrepreneur who was able to put passionate love behind what they built, *and* be able to successfully navigate it through the market. I believe one of the greatest examples of this paradigm was Apple Inc. CEO Steve Jobs.

Jobs used strategy and inspiration, synced them together and created one of the greatest companies the world has ever seen. You and I can employ the same means and reap similar results. It takes a mind committed to the process of reaching a similar level of achievement. We should simultaneously create, learn, tweak and create some more. As I emphasized earlier, our sole motivation should not be just to make money because that will limit us and stifle our creative passion. However, creating from a place of love and passionate inspiration (along with a desire for a greater income) can change the world.

Why Entrepreneurs Need to Be Good at Personal Money Management

The business world tends to make things more complicated than they need to be. I think it's just human nature to try to be prolific in areas that only require simplicity. Here's what I'm getting at: If you can manage a personal budget, you can deal with the complex numbers associated with running a company. It all comes down to expenses, revenues, profits and losses — it's that simple. Sure, there are very sophisticated accounting procedures done by chief financial officers, but at its core, you as the business owner only need to know the basics, especially when just starting out.

The only real difference between a personal budget and a business budget is the terms used on paper. For example, you may have laundry listed as an expense on your personal budget. A business statement may call it OPL (on premise laundry) on the expense report. Get familiar with the business terms associated with your niche, thus building your acumen, and learn how to see the similarities in your everyday life and those of your operation. I took several business math classes while in college, and the main things that I've needed to know in running a company are how to add, subtract, divide and multiply. Of course, there are variations and other types of equations used from time to time, but that's what Google is for, right?

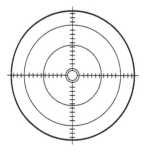

Scope of Accuracy – Google

Google is a company that has totally revolutionized the way we use the Internet. Basically, it's user-friendly search functionality-enabled Web navigation. In 2013, Web analytics company Alexa ranked Google.com as the most-visited website in the world. What started as a research project by two Ph.D. students — the company's founders Larry Page and Sergey Brin — has become a multinational conglomerate worth $395 billion as of 2014, second only to Apple for most valuable company in the United States. Google's mission since its inception has been to organize the world's information and make it universally accessible and useful. Here are a few things Google does to spur innovation and stay cutting edge:

- *Page and Brin have created a culture that rewards brilliance. Google hires the most gifted people it can find that fit well within the company.*

- *Twenty percent of the time, Googlers (Google employees) are expected to work on projects that interest them. As a result, products such as Gmail and AdSense were born.*
- *Google candidates go through a rigorous interview process before they are allowed to join the ranks.*
- *There are white boards all over Google offices. These allow Googlers to draw and write ideas in team settings, which helps spur creativity.*
- *Google is very efficient. In team meetings, it is common for Googlers to stand while holding an oversized pencil when it is a team member's turn to talk (time is limited to two minutes).*

The key to accuracy in the area of business finance is to keep things as simple as you possibly can and trust that you will be able to find the answers to your questions when they arise (because you will). That's how many of the pros approach it. Carlos Slim Helú, the billionaire telecommunications mogul, hardly ever uses a computer — he prefers just a paper and a pen. Lesson learned. He has harnessed the power of teamwork and surrounds himself with people much smarter than himself in this area.

Don't Burn Bridges (If You Can Help It)

You've probably heard the saying, "It's business, not personal." While it easier to adopt this idea in theory, it is hard to operate according to it in the heat of business conflict. The truth is, business can be very personal at times and it takes maturity and a thick skin to be successful. One thing that I wish I would have learned earlier in my business career was the principle of not burning bridges. A story is in order to provide context for what I'm getting at.

When I was in my early twenties, I was working on a venture that I was very passionate about. I had done this same project in years past, but the big difference this time was that I was working with a group of equally ambitious young men who were just as passionate about the undertaking as I was. We all started out with good intentions and no one was trying to get over on anyone else. Things were simple at first, but the further we moved along in the development of this project, the more complicated they became. At the time, I did not have the best advisers around me, and their counsel did more harm than good and probably escalated things more than they needed to be.

So there we were, some fledgling but motivated businessmen doing something we were very passionate about but not fully aware of how to carry it out. To say the least, mistrust began to form on both sides. I felt as if one side of the partnership had betrayed my trust especially when he brought in a new guy who, in my opinion, was untrustworthy. The other side probably felt like I was unpredictable and not true to my word. I'll admit, that is partly true because I was young and didn't have a good grasp on how to negotiate and talk deals out.

> *Humility goes a long way in business. The goal should never be just for one side to win, but all parties involved.*

Long story short, we ended up creating this great product but it never really gained its full momentum because it was sabotaged by our own immaturity and lack of experience. My sounding board suggested that I cut ties with them as soon as I could and that's what I did. To this day, I wonder what the possibilities could have been had I swallowed my pride and tried to work the arrangement out a little better for all sides. We all put a lot of our own personal resources into making this particular product great, but the bridge of communication was burned down, never to be crossed again.

I learned a very valuable lesson in this. Humility goes a long way in business. The goal should never be just for one side to win but all parties involved. Existing and developing expectations should be discussed as often as possible instead of everyone trying to hold their cards to their chest. The only time a bridge should be burned in business is if someone has a true character flaw and is intentional about screwing someone else over in the arrangement. Other than that, we may opt to forego a certain partnership if the numbers don't add up, but we should always leave a door open should a new opportunity present itself.

Business is really just a conglomerate of interwoven relationships seeking to advance both individually and collectively.

Get Good at Collaborating

An old adage asserts that two heads are better than one. There is a profound effect that occurs when two or more minds connect. Think of it like this: Most people find it easier to study around other students who are doing the same. Without any exchange of words, we can subconsciously draw on the energy of others to get to our desired goal. So imagine how great it can be if we worked in groups or teams actively communicating and bouncing ideas off one another.

Furthermore, we are able to gain access to the best of what other people have to offer when we forge together in entrepreneurial endeavors. Sadly, we find ourselves in an overly competitive and individualistic world that doesn't see things the same way. Yet, accuracy seems to put a demand on us to humble ourselves and take the greatest route that will lead to the best outcome.

There is sage wisdom in Proverbs 20:18, which advises us to obtain guidance before waging war. Proverbs 15:22 also says that plans succeed with many advisers. What does that mean for you and me? In order to succeed in business, we must get into the habit of picking the brains of other people and utilizing their wisdom to our advantage.

Make It Last, Make It Sustainable

Accurate entrepreneurs find a way to make their businesses grow and continue to flourish with or without them. The best enterprises are those that don't need the top person in order for it to function as it should. This does not make the chief visionary irrelevant. On the contrary, the role of the owner and/or CEO is to cast the vision. The people and resources set in place will ensure that the business gets to the desired destination time and time again. Once more, we find that we don't live in a world that operates according to this principle. We often find ourselves in a culture of CEO and/or business superstar worship. Should the founder die or leave, the stock often falls along with the company. Such was the case for Apple after Steve Jobs left in 1985 following a major clash with the board of directors.

However, I believe we witnessed a very powerful demonstration of sustainable operation through Apple once Jobs passed away. It's as if the company never missed a beat. It actually appears to be doing a bit better at the time of this writing. Its move to create Apple University and inject the DNA of Jobs and other core thinkers into the rest of the company was ingenious. We have yet to see the full ramifications of such a smart play by a masterfully strategic company.

It would be smart of us to try to somewhat duplicate this type of model, of course, according to our own scale and resources. We should get an early start in training culture champions who will push the overall vision to the other stakeholders in the company. With their buy-in, our firms can ascend heights impossible to even the most gifted and charismatic visionaries trying to do it alone.

Again, this takes humility and a willingness to lay our lives down. But we will find, as many wise business owners before us have, that we will attain greater peace, more time, and less stress as a result.

Be Open-Minded

We never know how unrelated events, experiences, career paths, and relationships will help us create a masterpiece in our line of work. Learn all that you can and allow yourself to have a wide range of interests outside of business. You will find that these will be great sources of creativity for your work. The more we expose ourselves to, the deeper our well of inspiration will be. I challenge you to take a class or read a magazine, or do some activity that is totally out of the norm for you. I bet you'll be surprised at the rush of new passion and vigor you'll have once you return to your regularly scheduled program.

Learn all that you can and allow yourself to have a wide range of interests outside of business. You will find that these will be great sources of creativity for your work.

Refuse to Become Complacent, Even While being Complacent

I know the above statement sounds like a contradiction, but hear me out. There are seasons in business (and life) where there is hardly any momentum. There's just a natural ebb and flow that occurs in any endeavor. Some months and years are great, others are so-so, and others are downright brutal. It is critical to develop the habit of continual movement, even when there doesn't seem to be much wiggle room in your circumstances. We can't always control what happens to us, but we can control how we react to what happens to us. We don't have to become complacent in our minds and actions, although everything around us appears to be frozen. Always keep learning and coming up with new plans and ideas. These will be a rich reservoir to draw upon once you have the power to act on your desires again.

Winter seasons in business (where hardly any of your efforts seem to bear any fruit) will eventually turn to spring again. Those who stay sharp during the winter and continue to sow the right seeds will see massive gains once the proverbial tide turns (and it always does). Accurate people are able to maintain an optimistic point of view in the face of a difficult reality. They forcefully press positive change upon their circumstances, instead of letting these circumstances dictate the outcome.

Complacency, or lack of movement, will kill you in business. Even if you don't know what to do, just do something. Often times, some sort of movement will help you find the answer that you need. Just standing still and waiting for things to get better can produce a mental paralysis that will make your situation worse.

Adopt an Explorer's Mindset

As we conclude our discussion on Business and Entrepreneurship, I want to leave you with this thought. Business, like life, is an unpredictable sport. It's a wild beast that is nearly impossible to control. Therefore, it is much better to have an explorer's mindset and keep tinkering until you find something that works consistently. Then once you find that, tinker some more because there will come a day when the rules change. We need to be ready to make the necessary adjustments.

Application of Accuracy

- **Remember that business is ultimately about relationships. Become a great relationship builder and you have a better chance at being successful.**
- **Do something that you are passionate about because your business is an extension of who you are.**
- **Don't be afraid to fail. The more you fail the more experience you gain. You will eventually get it right if you don't quit.**
- **Build something bigger than you. Create a company that can outlive you. That is a true legacy.**

Section IV

Health and Goals

Since our bodies are a temple, we should care for them as best as we possibly can. We are made of some of the most remarkable technology ever created. Learning to care for our minds, bodies and souls takes discipline, and those who pay the price will reap huge rewards in their later years. Without a goal, we have nothing to aim at — we are ships without a shore and there will never be an end to our means. The habit of goal setting is what sets the accurate apart from the average. This one small activity, done on a daily basis, provides motivation and an excitement for life that is difficult to find elsewhere.

CHAPTER 10

Health

An Inspiring Story

I had a very intriguing conversation with an older gentleman, probably in his early sixties, who looked like he had been around the block a few times but was still fit enough to run with the young bucks. I stood in his art gallery as he pointed out window shoppers whom he could tell were unhealthy probably because of the food they ate. I gave ear to this older gentleman's viewpoint on how poor diet habits are affecting the lives of millions of Americans. He referred to fast food as "poison" and went as far as to say that obesity and high blood pressure, especially in people of color, were as deadly as guns and missiles. He passionately spoke about food being used as a legal form of genocide and how if we are not careful, will kill people the same way violence is.

I did not necessarily agree with everything the gallery owner said during our conversation. However, I have learned how to eat the meat and spit out the bones when it comes to information. For a long time, I had the suspicion that fast food was detrimental to health. Yet, I was amazed at how many people would eat it, even when they knew it wasn't good for them. Isn't that just like eating poison that tastes good?

The majority of food manufacturers are for-profit companies that have large marketing budgets, sales quotas, aggressive CEOs, stock holders, thousands of employees, large facilities, and a host of other big-ticket items that send their overheads through the roof. They are not bad people or entities; however, our health is more than likely not their highest priority. They are in business to make money, take care of their families and live a reasonably comfortable existence. People generally buy what tastes good. Therefore, it makes very sound business sense to sell what your consumers want to buy even if it's unhealthy. If they don't, their competitors will, right?

The only problem is that the food that we crave is destroying us. It is reducing our quality of life and making many of us sick. We can't necessarily blame these food companies for our health woes because they are not forcing us to eat their products. Eating right and good health take intentional effort and planning. It doesn't just fall into our laps. How I wish it did.

It is very rare for someone to become wealthy on accident. Similarly, hardly anyone usually enjoys good health that lasts by happenstance either.

Creating Your Powerful 'Why' Factor for Accurate Health

It's an uphill battle these days if you are trying to be healthy. It appears that the current health care system, marketers, peers, family, and even our own mental conditioning work against us from gaining and maintaining optimal health. In certain cultures, you can be deemed arrogant or uppity if you are trying to be healthy. How wild is that? Therefore, we need to arm ourselves with powerful reasons why we do what we do in order to stand our ground against these endless waves of opposition.

As you get into the habit of repeating to yourself why you want to be healthy, your mind will be conditioned to withstand ideas, opinions and feedback that work against this goal.

I suggest writing out why you want to be healthy and reminding yourself of it on a daily basis. As you get into the habit of repeating to yourself why you want to be healthy, your mind will be conditioned to withstand ideas, opinions and feedback that work against this goal. I'll let you in on a little secret. My reason for wanting to have accurate health is because I have seen countless family members, including my father, suffer and die due to bad decisions made concerning their bodies. In my opinion, many in my family and immediate circle have died prematurely and did not maximize their full potential. Another reason why I want accurate health is because I want to live beyond my eighties and feel great as I age. I don't want to stick around if I'm rickety and decrepit as an old timer.

My plan is to be full of life, vigor, excitement and purpose in my latter years. These why statements are what help me to make wise choices when it comes to taking care of my body. Of course, I don't get it right all the time, but I am making progress. Continual progress is always much better than short-lived glory.

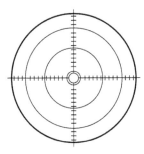

Scope of Accuracy – Kobe Bryant

Kobe Bryant knows a thing or two about accuracy. The five-time World Champion, 16-time All-Star, 15-time member of the All-NBA First Team, 12-time member of the All-Defensive First Team and four-time All-Star MVP has an unrelenting drive to be the best.

The only thing that's as impressive as his athletic ability and passion for the game is his longevity at an elite level. This has not come by accident. Bryant adheres to a strict diet of little to no sugar and he works out six hours a day, six days a week, six months out of the year. On average, he makes between 700 and 1,000 shots during his workout. These are not shots taken — these are shots made.

He understands that he's not as young as he used to be and there are more guys coming into the league who are younger and more athletic. Therefore, Bryant is in the gym at 6 a.m. "blacking out." Bryant doesn't call what he does working out, he calls it blacking out because he pushes himself past his previous limitations until he is very uncomfortable. Bryant is a strong proponent of stretching and he says that he is always learning new ways to improve his game.

He dubbed himself the "Black Mamba," the most poisonous snake in the world that strikes with 99 percent accuracy. When you watch him play, you see why the parallel is made. Bryant is still one of the most feared offensive players in the league, as well as one of the better defenders. Many of today's greatest players such as LeBron James and Kevin Durant mention Bryant when discussing who they look up to and who has had influence on their game.

A Gradual Shift

What's interesting is that our health issues are usually the result of bad habits that have developed over time. We will form some type of habit, whether it is good or bad. Positive habits take intentionality, negative ones form on autopilot. If we practice good habits long enough we will do them naturally.

What's more, the human tongue's taste buds change every day. It is our memory of what tastes good and bad that we have to be disciplined enough to change. Food companies spend billions of dollars on marketing trying to convince us to buy their products. There's nothing necessarily wrong with that. How will we know to buy a product if we are not aware that it exists? One could argue that these companies are coercive in their marketing campaigns. That may very well be true, but that still cannot be the excuse we use to justify the lack of discipline in our eating habits.

It is up to us to make wise choices. Spend some time listening to audio books or reading literature on health. Filling our minds with good information will give us the tools we need to make the best decision when a choice has to be made between one meal and another. I personally find that being aware of the right information helps me stay motivated to choose the path of accuracy. We are prone to go the wrong way if we don't have a strong enough reason to go in the right direction. It's harder to say no to a processed hamburger in a world filled with strategic, well-tested marketing if we don't know the type of complications eating this way can cause.

80-Year-Olds Who Look Better Than 50-Year-Olds

In their groundbreaking book, *Younger Next Year*, Chris Crowley and Dr. Henry S. Lodge discuss the importance that exercise plays in maintaining your health way into your eighties and beyond. One of the golden nuggets (and there are many) that I took from this writing is that even though everyone has to go through the aging process, that doesn't mean that everyone has to decay. There is a big difference between aging and decaying. We can gracefully age and feel great if we develop the habit of regular exercise at least six days a week.

That may sound like a big commitment, but think of it in terms of extending your body's warranty. Every time you take a brisk walk or jog, you're helping your body stay well conditioned, thus preserving its life. Think of all the things you could do if you could still operate at a high level well into your eighties and nineties. Imagine seeing your children's kids and their kids, and perhaps even their kids and being able to still play with them!

Exercise releases chemicals in the brain that empower the body to keep the process of decay at bay. If we couple that with good nutrition, stress reduction and spending more time doing things we love (with the people we love) we all can have a greater quality of life as we enter our golden years.

If You Don't Know What's in It, Don't Eat It

In his refreshingly controversial and witty book, *Doctor Yourself,* Dr. Andrew Saul cautions his readers to stay away from packaged foods that have unfamiliar ingredients in them. From several years of research, study and teaching, he has discovered that diets rich in fruits, vegetables and vitamin supplements, such as vitamin C, help ward off cancer and several other diseases that the medical industry has deemed incurable.

Saul courageously states that sick patients who rely on prescription drugs and other expensive treatments are more profitable to the health care industry than are healthy patients. A good medical practitioner is one who assists you to the point that you don't need him. The health care industry profits from disease; there is no benefit in prevention for them.

Read all labels on the back of the food you consume and if it's something you can't pronounce, stay away from it. As I stated earlier, money is the top priority for the majority of food companies and health care businesses. Therefore, we should be very aware of this and protect ourselves from getting caught in a web of bad health due to nutritional carelessness.

Natural Remedies

We have an innate tendency to overcomplicate simple things to our own harm. This could not be truer than in the area of medicine and medical treatment. It breaks my heart to see loved ones and other people who I care a great deal about taking several medications that supposedly solve one problem only to create severe side effects in other parts of the body.

Doctors are quick to prescribe harmful treatments that make already dire health conditions worse. I know that's not their intention and I don't want to paint them as the bad guy. Yet, there is a very fundamental flaw in the health care industry's approach to curing patients. While I do believe in following the doctor's advice in taking certain prescriptions in severe cases, this should not be the default treatment method.

God in all His eternal brilliance provides everything the human body would need in order to remain healthy. All of these natural remedies are much healthier and cheaper, and they work. Why wouldn't we want to take natural medicines that don't have any serious side effects? I can't think of any, can you? There are so many myths that are touted as true in the health care world. In order to be accurate in the area of health, we can't be lazy. It will require discipline to search out the correct information (which is very accessible) and apply that knowledge. It will be interesting to see how the Affordable Health Care Act shapes the future of the health care industry.

> *Taking natural vitamin supplements, as well as eating food strategically, can help ward off, limit and eradicate common diseases, such as diabetes, cancer, blindness and kidney disease.*

Taking natural vitamin supplements, as well as eating food strategically, can help ward off, limit and eradicate common diseases, such as diabetes, cancer, blindness and kidney disease. Think about it. Our world is so vast. There are so many different types of vegetation and minerals that have the solutions we need inside of them waiting to be discovered. If we understand this concept collectively, it will cause many financial problems for those in the health care industry that profit from disease. Perhaps that is why information regarding the powerful health enhancing benefits of vitamins doesn't get the same marketing dollars that prescription drugs do.

As Dr. Saul has said, there is no profit in prevention. Revenue is driven by disease in today's health care system. I truly believe that people are beginning to wake up though. The same way the housing bubble tanked and forced many people to reassess their financial lives, I believe that there is going to be a burst in the health care world that forces many people to scrutinize and pay closer attention to their eating and lifestyle habits. Armed with the proper knowledge, many people will be able to doctor themselves. The physicians and other health care professionals who will thrive in this foreseeable future will welcome patients that facilitate their own healing.

Those who stay stuck in the old way of prescribing drugs to their patients will go the way of the dinosaur. Better yet, the outdated method of doing things in the health care industry will be similar to what happened in the music industry post Napster and what is now happening in the automotive industry with companies not able to make the shift to electric vehicles and sustainable fuel.

Be Mindful of Health

I heard a surprising statistic that approximately 70 percent of all illnesses are stress related. Wow! Stress has more to do with our minds than most people know. We are literally worrying ourselves to death. I once heard a very wise person say that worry is a useless emotion because it does absolutely nothing to change the situation. Easier said than done, I know, but it is definitely worth a shot if people are dropping like flies because of this silent killer.

World-renowned minister and author Joyce Meyer quipped in her potent book, *Power Thoughts*, that it is impossible to think power-draining thoughts and then be powerful when situations arise that call for extra strength. I want to combine this thought with an idea presented by Drs. Mehmet Oz and Michael Roizen in their enlightening writing, *You Staying Younger*. In it, they cleverly draw parallels between the human body and a city, likening the brain to a city's electric power grid. It is the mechanism that gives juice to the entire city (or body). Without it, the city cannot function. Now reflect on Joyce Meyer's statement again.

Our power is drained by negative thinking. Worry often is the source of power drain to your body's electrical grid. These authors who differ as far as the east is from the west seem to find some common ground when it comes to how thinking affects our health. It's just as important to think healthy thoughts as it is to exercise and eat properly. To paraphrase Proverbs 23:7, as a person thinks so is he or she.

Energy

I remember the time when I had my first experience with a personal trainer. The guy was phenomenal and he was able to help his clients achieve amazing results by having them do things that were seemingly small. He personally impacted my life with his revolutionary concept of food, which helps me maintain focus to this day: He doesn't view food as a source of entertainment but as fuel to keep his body in optimal condition. Amazing, right? What if we all approached our diet with that outlook? What types of decisions would we make regarding what we put into our biological gas tank?

Food provides us with the critical fuel that we need to operate our physiological machinery. Some cars need premium gasoline while others are quite fine with regular unleaded. It is no different for the human body. Without the right gasoline in our system, we will end up on the side of the road somewhere waiting for assistance (think ambulances, walkers, wheelchairs, etc.). On the other hand, the right fuel will enable our bodies to work at their optimal level allowing us to reach peak performance.

I like the way Brian D. Biro put it in his life-changing book, *Beyond Success*. He sums up the impact that eating has on our energy level by saying, "A diet rich in fresh vegetables and fruits (especially homegrown and organically farmed), whole grains, legumes, fresh juice, pure water, and super foods loaded with natural trace minerals, amino acids, and chlorophyll is your best defense against disease and your greatest support for a strong and healthy immune system. It is fundamental to maintaining vibrant energy."

When your cell phone, computer or laptop has a drain on its battery, there isn't much you can do with them for a sustained period of time. It is necessary to keep these devices charged up in order to get the most use out of them. Again, we can draw a parallel to how our bodies function without energy. After all, energy is what allows us to work hard, love hard and play hard. It is essential if we're going to live a fulfilling life.

Laughter, Medicine for the Soul

Did you know that keeping a healthy sense of humor is good for your body? Laughter fires neurons in the brain, which actually help strengthen the immune system. People who don't take life too seriously end up enjoying it more and,

> *Laughter fires neurons in the brain, which actually help strengthen the immune system.*

guess what; there is a strong connection between liking your life and living longer.

Developing your comedic instincts can also help prohibit Alzheimer's disease and dementia because it improves cognitive function. You have to be mentally aware, sharp, and active to tell a good joke. So making people laugh causes you to use several key components of the brain simultaneously. Not to mention, a good chuckle with our buddies also fosters positive emotions, which in turn deepen our social bonds. Community with others is a crucial element for good health and longevity.

Folks that let life get the worst of them eventually lose their will to fight and have less reason to live. They typically push people away, thus alienating themselves from community, which is necessary for a healthy and well-balanced existence. Smiling and laughing more is attractive to people and draws them in for relationship building. That's what we need and want most in our lives. We absolutely need to be around people who love us, like us, and who we can share great times with.

This accuracy stuff is serious business, but that doesn't alleviate the need to laugh and enjoy your life regardless of how challenging the journey may be.

Know How Your Body Works

Perhaps one of the main reasons why so many people suffer from bad health is because they don't know how their body functions. God blessed us with some pretty fancy equipment and we would do well to learn as much as we can about it. I believe that we would have a greater appreciation for our body and all the components within it if we knew how it worked.

The human body has so many complex systems within it that do a fantastic job of keeping us healthy, if we give these systems what they need in order to be effective. Understanding how these systems work will give us an exciting challenge to get our bodies into tip-top shape and maintain that level.

Dr. Oz's *A Younger You* helps us understand how white blood cells are like club bouncers escorting good patrons into the party while simultaneously protecting against threats in the blood stream. Our genes are similar to a city's geography. There's little that a city can do to change its geographic location, but it can build its infrastructure in a way that minimizes risks and damages that are common to that region.

Most of the diseases running rampant in our society can be controlled by being smart when it comes to what we eat, how we think, how we handle stress, and exercise.

Soul Food

In all this talk about health, we cannot forget the importance of caring for our soul. Some health experts don't talk about care in this arena because it's not very tangible. But if we fail to look after our souls, it is only a matter of time before our physical quality of life diminishes. The soul is the part of us that lives on after we die. It is the vaulted database of our experience, memories, personality, and desire. In short, the soul characterizes who we are.

> *Every day that we get up and work — whether through physical, mental or spiritual labor — we give out energy that needs to be replenished consistently if we hope to have any longevity.*

It's easy to get caught up in the rat race of getting more money and buying bigger toys. This not only places wear and tear on our bodies and minds; it also takes its toll on our very essence, the soul. Jesus asked the thought-provoking question, what good is it for a man to gain the whole world yet lose his soul? The temptation to neglect our soul's well-being for temporary satisfaction is very strong. Perhaps that is why we see the decline of morals in every single facet of society.

Furthermore, we must keep our souls fit much like we keep our minds and bodies. We care for our soul by quiet reflection, vacationing, spending time with those we love, creating great memories and connecting with our Creator. I'm sure there are more ways, but these are a few that stick out to me as some of the most effective.

Reflection

It's important to reflect on your life. Drawing from the rich database of your experience from time to time will help you navigate your future. Seeing your past mistakes and successes enables you to view life through an objective lens. You will be able to ask yourself questions such as, "Is the direction I'm going leading to my desired destination?" There is nothing worse than going through life without coming up for air only to realize that you have been spent the last five to ten years swimming in the wrong direction.

Vacationing

Revisiting Stephen R. Covey's principle of "sharpening the saw" once more, we come to understand that rest is pertinent to replenishing one's creative energy and internal center. Every day that we get up and work — whether through physical, mental or spiritual labor — we give out energy that needs to be replenished consistently if we hope to have any longevity. Vacations allow us the time necessary to unwind and fill our physiological, mental and spiritual pipelines again.

Spending Time with Those We Love

I once heard someone say that when you lie on your death bed, you won't care about how much money you made or the expensive toys you acquired. What you will want most is to be close to the ones you love. Loving someone else deeply has huge health benefits. It gives us something greater to live for than ourselves. Having someone to care for has an amazing way of causing us to overcome health challenges and other tragedies.

Feelings of well-being (i.e. being loved by someone and loving them back) release chemicals in the brain that strengthen us physically. It's important to have people in your life who you're close to in an intimate way (this does not mean sex). A loving spouse, children, and friends are great people to display affection toward on a regular basis. The reciprocation of that love back to you has a great health benefit attached.

More Sex, Please

Did you know that having more sex can actually increase your likelihood of living longer? Isn't that fantastic news? Hold your horses, you wild stallion you. The kind of sex that I'm speaking of is that which is experienced in marriage. According to brain expert Dr. Amen (great name, don't you think?), men who have orgasms more frequently stand to live longer than men who don't. No wonder Marvin Gaye wrote the song "Sexual Healing." He was right on the money. Good sex releases chemicals in the pleasure area of the brain producing feelings of well-being and joy. These feelings of emotional ecstasy boost the immune system, physical endurance, and mental fortitude. Yes! So the next time your spouse tries to roll over on you when you're in the mood, let them know that it's a matter of life or death for you to engage in some good old-fashioned lovemaking. See if that works!

Learn Something New

A great way to stay sharp mentally is to be a lifelong learner. Treat your brain (one of the most important organs in your body) as a muscle and work it out as much as you can. Feed your mind great information, which will keep your brain active and improve your long-term quality of life. Take a crack at a new language, instrument, trade or work assignment. Pick something you enjoy that will be somewhat of a challenge for you. Master the new pursuit and then find something new to stimulate your mind. Our minds affect every aspect of our lives, so care for yours and continue to discover its potential.

Think Back on Health

Health, as many of us know, is a very broad topic covered in several exceptional books, so this portion of the book is meant to inspire you to dig deeper on your own while simultaneously offering a few ideas that you can hang your hat on. This will be a section of the book that is good to reference from time to time so the information stays fresh in your mind. We act on what we believe and we believe what information our minds are continuously washed with.

Application of Accuracy

- Create your powerful "why" factor that reminds you of why you want to be healthy. Remind yourself of it daily in order to withstand the influences trying to move you away from this goal.
- Watch what you eat on a regular basis. If you don't know what the food consists of, steer clear of it.
- Exercise regularly, every day if possible. Those who are active reduce the speed of the decaying process as we age.
- Spend time with loved ones and laugh often.
- Take regular vacations and reflect about life, your goals, and your faith.
- For the married folks only, have plenty of sex!

Chapter 11

Goals

What's Your Target?

As we come to close of this book, I hope to leave you with one of the most important pieces of information that pertains to accurate living. Accuracy is all about hitting the correct target. A target is something that an archer aims at, which implies that before she can hope to gauge effectiveness, there must be something in her range of motion to hit. One cannot be careless and be accurate. It takes hard work, intentionality and persistence to pierce the desired target.

Every area discussed in this writing will require us to do ongoing critical thinking, planning, and strategizing. It takes intentional action to make sure we're on track toward our goals. This isn't an easy feat, as you probably know. We are all too familiar with the fact that life throws unexpected curve balls every day and some of them are potent enough to paralyze us. The people in our environments are sometimes erratic and unpredictable, making it difficult to get to our desired progress. However, focus must be fixed on what we have control of and not on what we don't. We must learn how to adjust, and be mentally, physically and emotionally agile, while sticking to our guns when it comes to what God has placed in our heart.

Think Big

One of the critical success factors that I hear accurate entrepreneurs and business people cite often is the ability and commitment to think big. They aimed for goals that would really make their lives significant if they accomplished them. The majority of them refused to be mediocre; therefore, they would not let their thinking be a liability to their process.

Today, we look at people like Bill Gates, Richard Branson and Warren Buffett because of their amazing wealth, accomplishments, and accuracy in their industries. Yet, in order to get where they are, it had to start with them having a big vision. Gates had the behemoth goal of seeing a personal computer on every desk in America and creating software easy enough for his mother to use. Consider that at the time he was starting out, one computer took up a whole room. People probably thought he didn't take his medication when he told them what he thought was possible because it hadn't been done before.

Accuracy is usually a path that must be trail-blazed or rediscovered because of the muddied waters and pathways littered with garbage hiding it. The murkiness comes in the form of thought systems that have become socially acceptable (but are totally inaccurate) and pervasive throughout culture. In many spheres today, mediocrity is widely accepted. Yet, big thinkers tend to be uncomfortable living within the traditional bounds their surroundings try to place on them. Those who think big and follow those thoughts with big action stand out from the crowd. Accuracy seekers must be willing to be looked at as abnormal. They are, in fact, creating and recreating the new normal.

> *We must learn how to adjust, and be mentally, physically and emotionally agile, while sticking to our guns when it comes to what God has placed in our heart.*

Write Your Goals Down

Self-made millionaire and author Joe Karbo said, "People who have written goals tend to live up to them; those who don't drift." Once more, he wisely states, "Without clear, well-defined goals, success is impossible." These powerful statements struck me when I read them. How could something so simple produce such high level returns? Part of the reason is that writing down your goals gives both the conscience and subconscious parts of your mind somewhere to direct its energy. Our brains are the greatest piece of technology ever invented. Written goals are like software loaded into our hard drive. Our systems naturally make the necessary connections and computations needed in order for that software to put out the correct outputs. That's my nerdy way of saying we will move toward the direction of where we focus our attention.

I mentioned earlier in the book the importance of using affirmations. Karbo suggests the same, saying that our "goals should become daily declarations." Speak them in the present tense as if already living in the reality of them. This reinforces their realness to you (writing them down has already made them substantially more tangible).

We've discussed several ways that accuracy can and should look for our lives throughout this book. I strongly suggests taking some time right now to think of the areas you desire to be accurate in and write down how that will play out in your life. For example, you may write an affirmation goal for your health like:

"I am a very healthy person who eats well-balanced meals consisting of fruits, vegetables, lean meats, tea and water. I enjoy being healthy and at my best every day. I have a tremendous amount of energy that is the result of exercising four days out of the week, limiting stress, following a well-planned and enjoyable diet, and having a lot of fun in life."

Reciting this affirmation daily for 40 days or more will cement it in your mind and make this an automatic goal that you naturally move toward. It may seem farfetched and unrealistic in the beginning, but what you are doing is teaching your mind the way you want it to think and process the information it receives. Anything not in line with this way of thinking will quickly be discarded and you will find yourself only taking actions that make this your reality. We eventually become what we fix our mind on.

Karbo asserts, "You find some things that you really thought you wanted, you really don't. … Working through your goals this way tends to isolate and highlight what really matters to you."

Take the Time to Set Your Goals

The greatest enemy of goal setting is busyness. The adage is, we are planning to fail if we fail to plan. You have to plan your accuracy — it will not just happen. If happenstance accuracy were the case, there wouldn't be such a miniscule number of people who reach it. We admire the Tiger Woods', Kobe Bryants, Michael Jordans, Oprah Winfreys, Warren Buffets, and Steve Jobs' of our world because of the accuracy they've been able to demonstrate in their given spheres of influence. These very busy people took time out of their schedule in order to become great at what they do. These people are no different than you and I in terms of the time they have available to them. We all have the same 24 hours in a day allotted to us to be just as productive.

Prioritize

The fruit of a person's life is the sum total of their priorities. Our priorities define us and shape our future. The college student who focuses on studying and doing homework correctly will reap the 4.0 GPA, magna cum laude status. On the reverse, the college student whose idea of studying is make-out sessions, mosh pits and hangovers probably won't get very far in their college career.

Prioritizing is a key to accuracy because it helps us segment our goals into bite-sized pieces that enable us to obtain them. Creating a list of what's most important will give us the sense of direction we need.

Keep Good People around You

Let me put a disclaimer out there about this subject matter. When I say "good people" I'm referring to people who are good for you. I really believe that modern culture is so quick to write people off as good or bad, and we are changing all the time. There are plenty of good people out there who aren't necessarily good for you as it relates to where you're trying to go. Nonetheless, they are great people and bring a tremendous amount of benefit to the people with whom they're supposed to connect.

Now that I cleared that up, I want to stress the importance of finding people who complement you, challenge you to become better, and bring the best out of you. These are the types of people you want to identify and be intentional about developing relationships with. The saying "you are the company you keep" is very true and we should pay close attention to it.

I've personally found that many counterfeits come before the real thing. There have been many times when I thought a love interest, friend, mentor, business opportunity, and so on and so forth was the one, only to find out that it wasn't, leaving very disappointed and sometimes devastated. I've learned to test the mettle of those who I closely associate with because their voice has a very strong influence in my life. The ideas and suggestions that get put into our head by those in our inner circle are powerful. I don't advocate being suspicious of people, but I strongly believe in carefully observing people's patterns and weighing motives and intentions.

The right circle of friends and associates can take you to places you have only dreamed of. Their wealth of knowledge, experiences, connections and other resources may be the very items you need to catapult to the next level of accuracy. Therefore, we should all be open to the qualified voices in our lives, treat them very well, and let them know how much we value them on a consistent basis.

Cut Out as Much Distraction as Possible

Who loves distraction? I do! I swear it's worse than crack cocaine for some of us. I often joke with friends that I am addicted to my smart phone. I catch myself checking my Facebook and other social media sites every 30 seconds. It's so automatic. I reveal all this top secret information to let you know that it's normal to allow yourself to get distracted. It's just part of human nature. We're curious beings and whatever we're not focusing on always appears to be more interesting than the task at hand. However, in order to be accurate, that good old "D" word that many of us hate has to be put into effect repetitively. That word is none other than discipline. Accurate people learn how to cut out distraction so that they can give the majority (if not all) of their energy toward what they are working on. The bad news is that it will only get harder to be disciplined in this time of instant access to just about anything you want. The good news is that this allows us the tremendous opportunity to set ourselves a part and be accuracy leaders because of our commitment to being disciplined to obtain results.

So what are some clever ways we can cut out distraction? Well, there are myriad answers to that question. For starters, ask yourself what takes up most of your time that isn't helping you get closer to your goals (spouses, kids and chores don't count — ha!). Perhaps you watch too much TV, surf the Web with no aim in mind, get into other people's business, so on and so forth. These are the distractions that more than likely are causing you to miss your targets in life. So one thing that must be done is to recognize what's holding you back. The next thing to do is get some accountability in that area. For example, let your wife know that you are trying to capture certain goals in a particular area and that the TV is a hindrance to you reaching them (I'm sure she'll be glad to help). Ask her to lovingly nag you whenever you sit in front of the idiot box for more than an hour. Sure, you'll be annoyed and irritated on some days, but you'll be much happier in the long run after you become more accurate in the desired area.

I have mentioned creating a powerful "why" factor throughout this book. It is very helpful to employ this tool in this instance especially. Write down the benefits of becoming accurate and keep that sheet of paper in front of you daily. You may even want to post it on the items that are causing the distraction so you are reminded to refocus. The "why" factor's we develop remind us to get back on track. So we can sum up the three ways to cut out distraction as discipline, accountability, and our "why" factor. I'm sure there are plenty of other ways to knock out distraction but this is just a starting point.

Work Your Butt Off

My motto as of late has been "pray like it all depends on God, work like it all depends on you." In His infinite wisdom, God saw fit to partner with mankind as it pertains to realizing our full potential. He gives us gifts, talents, and abilities but it is up to us to put them to good use. Find what you're passionate about, seek God for His vision regarding it, and then get to work on it. If you have written out your goals as suggested above, you have a huge chance of accomplishing what you set out to do.

Most people don't like to work hard. Better yet, they don't want to risk failing so they play it safe. Perhaps they will work hard for their employer or someone else who they report to, yet no time is spent and no effort given toward their true purpose. This is inaccurate. We all have a God-given mandate to fulfill. It's usually connected to something that we're passionate about. We must get over the fear of failing (those who persist will never fail to reach their goals) and give our vision of accuracy everything we got.

I like how Oswald Chambers put it. He says very matter-of-factly, "All efforts of worth and excellence are difficult." That phrase can be discouraging to some, but to those who have the desire to rise above mediocrity into a place of sustainable greatness, these words are high-octane fuel. It lets us know what we are signing up for at the gate. The reason why so few people position themselves for accuracy is because it takes pure, good old-fashioned hard work. It takes resilience and persistence even when great setbacks occur.

> *Accurate people learn how to cut out distraction so that they can give the majority (if not all) of their energy toward what they are working on.*

Mental toughness and sturdiness of spirit are prerequisites for living an accurate life. You will constantly be challenged, criticized, discouraged and come against difficult circumstances. However, if you hang in there, I guarantee that you'll see your reality line up with your vision. *Rich Dad Poor Dad* author Robert Kiyosaki said it this way: "If you can learn to expect disappointment, yet move on regardless toward your goals, your success, even though it won't seem like it at the time, is virtually assured."

The work becomes hard when we are in the middle of challenging circumstances. Sticking out from the herd goes against our natural human tendency. Many people will not understand your vision, so they will criticize and mock you because that's what people tend to do when they don't understand things. Some people will just flat out ignore your efforts and not be interested. We must overcome the bitter emotions that this dynamic can produce. And we must remain diligent without carrying chips on our shoulders. Sometimes you'll temporarily hold a grudge until you learn to adjust mentally, forgive, and focus on the path of accuracy once again. But you can do it!

Accuracy, a Plan, Not Perfection

Accuracy does not mean perfection. It means aligning ourselves with God and his plan for our lives. There may be no fanfare in your lifetime or you may experience the best life has to offer. In the long run, this is not important. The priority is hearing God say, "well done," when we breathe our last breath and close our eyes to this side of eternity. So as you grow in accuracy, remain vigilant and encouraged. Maximize your potential and fulfill the destiny the Heavenly Father has planted in your heart. I know that you will do great things and be the model of accuracy this world so desperately needs.

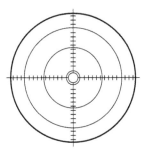

Scope of Accuracy – You

As we come to the end of this book, it is only the beginning of your journey. We've looked at many lives throughout this reading who have demonstrated accuracy in various areas. I want you to take a moment to think about what you want your legacy to be. Where do you desire to demonstrate accuracy, and who will benefit from this decision? It doesn't have to be grandiose either. Perhaps you simply what to be an accurate wife or husband, mother or father, mentor or friend. Even if you are not on the world's stage, the accuracy that you demonstrate will send ripples throughout the generations that follow you. So, I want you to write out what your accurate legacy will be in the space provided below. Revisit it from time to time to measure how you are shaping up.

Recommended Reading

Multiple Streams of Income — Robert G. Allen
Beyond Success — Brian D. Biro
50 Prosperity Classics — Tom Butler-Bowdon
My Utmost for His Highest — Oswald Chambers
The 5 Love Languages — Gary Chapman
Integrity — Henry Cloud
The 7 Habits of Highly Effective People — Stephen R. Covey
Younger Next Year — Chris Crowley and Dr. Henry S. Lodge
A Significant Life —Jim Graff
The Holy Bible — God
Growing a Business — Paul Hawken
The Millionaire Real Estate Investor — Gary Keller
Rich Dad Poor Dad — Robert Kiyosaki
The 17 Indisputable Laws of Teamwork — John C. Maxwell
The 21 Irrefutable Laws of Leadership — John C. Maxwell
Practicing Greatness — Reggie McNeal
Power Thoughts — Joyce Meyer
You Staying Younger — Dr. Mehmet Oz and Michael Roizen
Total Money Makeover — Dave Ramsey
StrengthsFinder 2.0 — Tom Rath
Doctor Yourself — Dr. Andrew Saul
Emotionally Healthy Spirituality — Peter Scazzero
The Leader Who Had No Title — Robin Sharma
The Millionaire Mind — Thomas J. Stanley
The Art of War — Sun Tzu
Leading From Your Strengths — John Trent, Rodney Cox and Eric Tooker

For more REBEL Firm content, visit rebelfirm.com.

To book Philip "Sharp Skills" Jacobs to speak or perform at your event, contact rebelbusiness@gmail.com.

To purchase Sharp Skills' music, visit sharpskillsmusic.com.

Connect with Philip "Sharp Skills" Jacobs on social media:

twitter.com/sharpskills24

facebook.com/sharpskillstherebel

CPSIA information can be obtained
at www.ICGtesting.com
Printed in the USA
FFHW020645260219
50707248-56100FF